Adult Bible Stud

Winter 2021–2022 • Vol. 29

Editorial and Design Team
Jan Turrentine, Editor
Tonya Williams, Production Editor
Keitha Vincent, Designer

Administrative Team
Rev. Brian K. Milford,
President and Publisher
Marjorie M. Pon, Associate Publisher
and Editor, Church School Publications

ADULT BIBLE STUDIES (ISSN 0149-8347): An official resource for The United Methodist Church approved by the General Board of Discipleship and published quarterly by Cokesbury, The United Methodist Publishing House, 2222 Rosa L. Parks Blvd., Nashville, Tennessee 37228. Copyright © 2021 by Cokesbury. Send address changes to ADULT BIBLE STUDIES, 2222 Rosa L. Parks Blvd., Nashville, Tennessee 37228.

To order copies of this publication, call toll free: 800-672-1789. FAX your order to 800-445-8189. Telecommunications Device for the Deaf/Telex Telephone: 800-227-4091. Automated order system is available after office hours. Or order through Cokesbury.com. Use your Cokesbury account, American Express, Visa, Discover, or MasterCard.

For permission to reproduce any material in this publication, call 615-749-6268, or write to Permissions Office, 2222 Rosa L. Parks Blvd., Nashville, Tennessee 37228. Scripture quotations in this publication, unless otherwise indicated, are from the Common English Bible, copyright 2011. Used by permission.

ADULT BIBLE STUDIES is designed to help adults understand the meaning and authority of the Bible for Christian life. Daily study helps are published in *Daily Bible Study*. Leadership helps are published in *Adult Bible Studies Teacher*, and at AdultBibleStudies.com.

Cover photo: Shutterstock

Meet the Writer

Gary Thompson

Gary Thompson is a retired ordained elder in the Mississippi Annual Conference of The United Methodist Church. Gary received his undergraduate degree from Delta State University in Cleveland, Mississippi, and an MRE from Southern Seminary in Louisville, Kentucky. He did additional study at New Orleans Seminary and Memphis Theological Seminary. He earned a DMin in leadership development from Princeton Theological Seminary.

Gary enjoys traveling. He is most proud of his wife, Robin; three children; and seven grandchildren. You can email Gary at *drgaryt@gmail.com*, follow him on Twitter at *@drgaryt*, or read his blog at *http://transformative church.blogspot.com/*.

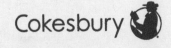
Cokesbury

Editorial and Design Team

Jan Turrentine, Editor

Tonya Williams Production Editor

Kellie Vincent, Designer

Administrative Team

Roy Branch, Million,

Creation and Publisher,

Marjorie M. Pon, Associate Publisher

and Editor, Church School Publications

Meet the Writer

Mary Thompson

Contents

Editor's Perspective

When did you last encounter something so amazing, so awe-inspiring, that you became momentarily breathless and your heart seemed to skip a beat? What did you see or hear or experience that filled you with absolute wonder?

That seems not to happen to us much these days, does it? Have we lost our capacity for awe and wonder? Are we so accustomed to the routineness of discoveries and inventions and technology and progress that we have become desensitized to feeling much of anything at all? And, worse, has our spiritual vision become dimmed to God's activity around us?

God's wonders have not ceased. Rather, wrote theologian Dietrich Bonhoeffer, "God travels wonderful ways with human beings, but . . . does not go the way that people want to prescribe; rather, his way is beyond all comprehension . . . [God] confounds the reason of the reasonable. . . . Only the humble believe him and rejoice that God is so free and so marvelous that he does wonders where people despair, that he takes what is little and lowly and makes it marvelous. And that is the wonder of all wonders, that God loves the lowly. . . . God marches right in. He chooses people as his instruments and performs his wonders where one would least expect them. God is near to lowliness; he loves the lost, the neglected, the unseemly, the excluded, the weak and broken."[1]

The big, the loud, the magnificent happenings naturally and easily grab our attention. They are difficult to ignore. It takes intention, however, to look toward rather than away from places of weakness, powerlessness, and hopelessness. But it is in those places that God is at work. A young, unmarried teenager. A faithful but bewildered and otherwise unknown carpenter. A crowded stable. A feed trough.

Part of the beauty of Advent is its call to wait, to pause in the stillness and the silence and allow our spiritual vision to readjust to the quiet activity of God in our midst. Our lessons this quarter, written by Gary Thompson, encourage that pause and then invite us to celebrate with wonder God's activity around us. And wonder of all wonders, God invites us to become involved.

"Give thanks to the only one who makes great wonders" (Psalm 136:4).

Jan Turrentine

Jan Turrentine
AdultBibleStudies@cokesbury.com

---

[1]From *God Is in the Manger: Reflections on Advent and Christmas*, by Dietrich Bonhoeffer (quoted at *goodreads.com*).

Daily Bible Readings (Unit 1)

November 29
1 Samuel 1:9-11

November 30
Numbers 9:15-23

December 1
Hebrews 11:13-16

December 2
Habakkuk 2:1-3

December 3
Revelation 6:9-11

December 4
James 5:7-11

December 5
Luke 1:5-25, 57-58

December 6
Psalm 40:1-5

December 7
Psalm 48:9-11

December 8
Psalm 73

December 9
Ecclesiastes
12:9-14

December 10
Exodus 3:1-3

December 11
Psalm 8:1-5

December 12
Luke 1:26-38,
46-55

December 13
2 Corinthians
4:16-17

December 14
Isaiah 46:3-4

December 15
Psalm 92:12-14

December 16
Proverbs 13:9-12

December 17
Psalm 71:18-19

December 18
Luke 12:35-40

December 19
Luke 2:25-38

December 20
Psalm 86:14-17

December 21
1 Peter 3:18-22

December 22
Psalm 103:6-14

December 23
2 Peter 3:8-10

December 24
Psalm 145:4-9

December 25
Romans 9:22-24

December 26
Revelation 3:20–
4:11

Unit 1
Wait for It

In his book *God Is in the Manger*, Dietrich Bonhoeffer wrote, "Celebrating Advent means being able to wait. Waiting is an art that our impatient age has forgotten. It wants to break open the ripe fruit when it has hardly finished planting the shoot. But all too often greedy eyes are only deceived; the fruit that seemed so precious is still green on the inside, and disrespectful hands ungratefully toss aside what has so disappointed them.

Whoever does not know the austere blessedness of waiting—that is, of hopefully doing without—will never experience the full blessing of fulfillment. Those who do not know how it feels to struggle anxiously with the deepest questions of life, of their life, and to patiently look forward with anticipation until the truth is revealed, cannot even dream of the splendor of the moment in which clarity is illuminated for them. For the greatest, most profound, tenderest things in the world, we must wait."[1]

In the four lessons in this unit, we examine the stories of those who recognized the importance of waiting on God's timing. Advent is altogether an appropriate season for such a study. Advent is indeed a season of waiting and anticipation.

In our first lesson, we read about Elizabeth and Zechariah, an elderly couple who had waited many years to have a much desired child. In Lesson 2, we recall the story of Mary and her unexpected pregnancy.

In the following lesson, we meet two others who faithfully waited most of their lives to see the promised Messiah. Our final lesson in this unit explores a text from the Book of Revelation that encourages us to reflect upon how God and Jesus wait for us.

[1]From *goodreads.com*.

Focal Passage: Luke 1:5-25, 57-58
Background Text: Luke 1
Purpose Statement: To recognize the importance of waiting on God's timing

Luke 1:5-25; 57-58

⁵During the rule of King Herod of Judea there was a priest named Zechariah who belonged to the priestly division of Abijah. His wife Elizabeth was a descendant of Aaron. ⁶They were both righteous before God, blameless in their observance of all the Lord's commandments and regulations. ⁷They had no children because Elizabeth was unable to become pregnant and they both were very old. ⁸One day Zechariah was serving as a priest before God because his priestly division was on duty. ⁹Following the customs of priestly service, he was chosen by lottery to go into the Lord's sanctuary and burn incense. ¹⁰All the people who gathered to worship were praying outside during this hour of incense offering. ¹¹An angel from the Lord appeared to him, standing to the right of the altar of incense. ¹²When Zechariah saw the angel, he was startled and overcome with fear.

¹³The angel said, "Don't be afraid, Zechariah. Your prayers have been heard. Your wife Elizabeth will give birth to your son and you must name him John. ¹⁴He will be a joy and delight to you, and many people will rejoice at his birth, ¹⁵for he will be great in the Lord's eyes. He must not drink wine and liquor. He will be

filled with the Holy Spirit even before his birth. [16]He will bring many Israelites back to the Lord their God. [17]He will go forth before the Lord, equipped with the spirit and power of Elijah. He will turn the hearts of fathers back to their children, and he will turn the disobedient to righteous patterns of thinking. He will make ready a people prepared for the Lord."

[18]Zechariah said to the angel, "How can I be sure of this? My wife and I are very old."

[19]The angel replied, "I am Gabriel. I stand in God's presence. I was sent to speak to you and to bring this good news to you. [20]Know this: What I have spoken will come true at the proper time. But because you didn't believe, you will remain silent, unable to speak until the day when these things happen."

[21]Meanwhile, the people were waiting for Zechariah, and they wondered why he was in the sanctuary for such a long time. [22]When he came out, he was unable to speak to them. They realized he had seen a vision in the temple, for he gestured to them and couldn't speak. [23]When he completed the days of his priestly service, he returned home. [24]Afterward, his wife Elizabeth became pregnant. She kept to herself for five months, saying, [25]"This is the Lord's doing. He has shown his favor to me by removing my disgrace among other people." . . .

[57]When the time came for Elizabeth to have her child, she gave birth to a boy. [58]Her neighbors and relatives celebrated with her because they had heard that the Lord had shown her great mercy.

Key Verse: "The angel said, 'Don't be afraid, Zechariah. Your prayers have been heard. Your wife Elizabeth will give birth to your son and you must name him John'" (Luke 1:13).

As I began writing this series of lessons, I, like you, was experiencing life differently than ever before. Many aspects of my daily existence were on hold. I was instructed to stay away from others. My church was shut down—no gatherings of any kind. Millions of people around the world became ill; and, sadly, many of them subsequently died.

We were in the midst of an international COVID-19 coronavirus pandemic. No one was sure how or when it would all end. You know much more about it now as you read this than I did at the time I wrote it.

I've never been a patient person. I have always halfway jokingly said I was afraid to pray for patience; I probably wouldn't like the things God would do to answer my prayer. Our modern technology certainly doesn't help.

We are used to getting what we want quickly. We eat instant potatoes and drink instant coffee. We flip a switch, and the darkness is instantly dispelled. News from around the world is promptly available to us 24/7. Internet search engines answer our questions in a matter of seconds. And if we want to see it for ourselves, we can go pretty much anywhere in the world in a matter of hours. But we know some things still take time.

A while back, one of my friends on social media was celebrating the fact that his century plant (*Agave americana*) was blooming. This was indeed something he had been looking forward to for many years. It is called a century plant because people once believed it bloomed only once in its lifetime. Now we understand it can take decades (though not a 100 years) to do so.

The once-in-a- lifetime bloom is quite spectacular. The huge bud is in the same family as asparagus and looks like a giant asparagus spear. Once the plant decides to bloom, the bud shoots up into the air at the phenomenal rate of five to seven inches per day.

God's creation is full of lessons like this. We are reminded that many of the best things in life take time and take place in God's timing, not ours.

Celebrating the Advent of Jesus

This is the first Sunday in Advent. The word *advent* is derived from the Latin *adventus*, which means "coming" or "arrival" (*ad*="add" or "plus"; *venire*="to come"). Beginning four Sundays before Christmas, Advent guides Christians to prepare thoughtfully for the celebration of Jesus' birth at Christmas and to wait expectantly for Christ's return at the Second Coming.

We look back with thanksgiving and look forward with faith and hope. Of course, while we wait for Christ's return, we are keenly aware his Spirit has never left us. Advent is a time of reflection, anticipation, and celebration.

Jesus' birth narrative is found only in the Gospels of Matthew and Luke. The details included in each account are quite different, as is the tone. Since the author of Matthew wanted to convince his primarily Jewish audience Jesus was the long-expected Messiah, he began with a genealogy of Jesus that revealed his connection with King David. He told the story of the magi who came to worship the new King, whose birth had been announced by the stars.

The author of Luke's Gospel wanted to show Jesus was not just the Jewish Messiah, but is in fact the Savior of the whole world, especially the weak and the vulnerable, who had little in the way of material assets. He related the story of John the Baptizer and highlighted the role of Mary, a poor young girl no one would ever have expected to be the mother of a king. Luke mentioned no magi but described poor shepherds coming to visit the Baby Jesus.

Before Luke tells us about Jesus' birth, he offers an extended account of John's birth. He begins that narrative by first telling us about John's parents, Zechariah and Elizabeth, who had spent much of their lives longing for a child.

This is a repeated theme in Scripture. Sarai, Abram's wife, was in her 90s before God finally gave her Isaac. Rebekah and Isaac were married 20 years before she gave birth to her twins, Jacob and Esau. Rachel, Jacob's wife, was childless for many years before finally giving birth to Joseph and Benjamin. Samson's mother was without a child until God finally answered her fervent prayers. Samuel's mother, Hannah, was also childless and wanted a son so badly, she promised to offer him to God in service.

In biblical times, it was considered a personal tragedy for a woman to be childless. It was also a shame for her not to give her husband a child.

How does Advent challenge you to examine your relationships with God and others? Is there barrenness or brokenness in your life? Is there something in your life that needs to change?

Waiting for God's Promises to Be Fulfilled

Three main characters appear in this text: Zechariah, Elizabeth, and the angel Gabriel. We know another main character, the powerful King Herod, lurked menacingly in the background (Matthew 2). Luke tells us Zechariah and Elizabeth "were both righteous before God, blameless in their observance of all the Lord's commandments and regulations" (Luke 1:6). While childlessness was often considered in ancient times to be a punishment by God—even grounds for divorce—our text makes it clear this was not the case with Zechariah and Elizabeth.

Herod, on the other hand, was infamous for his evil deeds. Matthew tells us this wicked man ordered the massacre of all male children under two years of age when he heard of Jesus' birth. While some historians question whether this massacre actually happened, most agree Herod was indeed a tyrannical ruler.

Perhaps the best indication of what people generally thought about Herod was expressed by Macrobius, an ancient Roman writer. In his book *Saturnalia*, he famously claimed when the Emperor Augustus heard Herod had ordered his own son be killed, the ruler quipped, "It is better to be Herod's pig than his son."[1]

Zechariah was a priest, meaning he was a direct descendant of Aaron, Moses' brother. Since every male descendant of Aaron was considered a priest, there were far more priests than needed. Therefore, they were formed into 24 units, each responsible for Temple duties twice each year. The lot system was used to determine who was chosen to perform specific duties. On this particular occasion, Zechariah had been selected to go into the Temple to burn incense. No doubt, he would have been overjoyed and would have considered himself fortunate to have been chosen.

While Zechariah went into the inner Court of the Priests, the others had to stay in the outer Court of the Israelites. The congregants waited for Zechariah and were surprised he had taken so much longer than usual to carry out his duties. The early verses of Luke's Gospel feature a great deal of waiting, something we will see throughout the lessons in this unit.

Zechariah and his wife, Elizabeth, had waited years for a child. The people waited for Zechariah. Zechariah went home after his experience in the Temple, but he still had to wait for his voice to be restored. And he had to wait even longer for God's promise to materialize.

In Lesson 3, we will consider Luke's account of two other people who had waited most of their lives to see the promised Messiah.

Do you agree with theologian Dietrich Bonhoeffer, who said, "For the greatest, most profound, tenderest things in the world, we must wait"?²

Don't Be Afraid; Your Prayers Have Been Heard

God sent the angel Gabriel to this humble, righteous priest with an important message: "Don't be afraid, Zechariah. Your prayers have been heard" (Luke 1:13). Right now, for me, these are powerful words indeed. As my family, friends, and even the whole international community are experiencing perhaps the scariest time of our lives, these words bring great comfort.

Zechariah would have been familiar with Hebrew Scripture. These words from the angel may well have reminded him of the words of the psalmist that have also recently brought comfort to me: "Even when I walk through the darkest valley, I fear no danger because you are with me. Your rod and your staff—they protect me" (Psalm 23:4). For a couple who wants children, to be childless can indeed be a dark valley. Moreover, a spiritual encounter with a heavenly being could certainly be a frightening experience.

Later in this chapter, Luke tells us Gabriel also said to Mary, "Don't be afraid" (Luke 1:30). In Chapter 2, we read where the angel announced Jesus' birth to the terrified shepherds, and he began with this same greeting (2:10).

Many of us don't think much about fearing God. Our emphasis is much more on loving God. Later in this chapter, Mary praises God and says, "For he that is mighty hath done to me great things; and holy is his name. And his mercy is on them that fear him from generation to generation" (1:49-50, KJV).

Here, the word translated "fear" is the Greek word *phobeomai*, a form of the word *phobos*. While this word means "to put in fear, terrify, or frighten," it also means "to reverence, to give honor or respect." This is surely what Mary is primarily talking about. In fact, the Common English Bible renders this verse, "He shows mercy to everyone, from one generation to the next, who honors him as God" (verse 50).

Of course, historically, most Christians have believed we need to fear God's judgment. I was recently watching National Geographic's series *The Story of God, With Morgan Freeman*. This particular episode was on heaven and hell. It concludes with Freeman suggesting many religions use the notion of heaven and hell to encourage people to do good and to avoid evil. It is understandable that an encounter with a divine being who has the power to punish with eternal damnation could be a frightening experience.

What kind of experiences have you had with God? Were those experiences frightening, comforting, challenging, or perplexing?

The Secret of Patient Waiting

The Jewish people had been waiting for God to send them a savior for many years. Of course, Jesus turned out to be a different messiah from the one they had been expecting. They had been praying for a savior much like the ones we read about in the Book of Judges. They had been waiting for the one who would run the despised Romans out of the country and restore the Davidic kingdom, the one prophesied, for example, in Zechariah 9:9: "Rejoice greatly, Daughter Zion. Sing aloud, Daughter Jerusalem. Look, your king will come to you. He is righteous and victorious." The victory was assumed to be over their earthly enemies.

Luke sets the stage for Jesus' birth by first relating the story of John, the primary character who would announce the birth of this different Messiah. Luke builds the anticipation of Jesus' birth in a dramatic fashion by telling a number of "waiting stories."

The church has now waited over 2,000 years for the second coming of Jesus Christ. Some have given up hope he will ever return. Perhaps the most pressing question for us to ponder during this Advent season is, How do we wait patiently but faithfully?

One day many years ago when I was in seminary, I walked by a doctoral student's office in the school library. He had taped a clipping of a cartoon to his door. In the pictures, a group of Christians was standing around looking up to heaven. Jesus approached them and asked, "What are you folks doing?"

"Oh," they answered, "we are waiting on Jesus to return."

You could see the disappointment on the Lord's face as he responded, "Is that what I asked you to do while waiting?"

I once read somewhere, "The secret of patience is doing something else in the meanwhile."

In John 14, Jesus says, "Don't be troubled. Trust in God. Trust also in me. . . . When I go to prepare a place for you, I will return and take you to be with me so that where I am you will be too" (John 14:1, 3). But Jesus didn't intend for us to sit around and simply wait. He gave us plenty to do.

Jesus repeatedly calls us to take up our cross and follow him (Matthew 16:24-26; Mark 8:34; Luke 9:23). He asked us to feed the hungry and clothe the naked (Matthew 25). He commissioned us to go into all the world and make disciples (Matthew 28:16-20).

Jesus insisted that his disciples are all called to be servants. "Jesus called [the Twelve] over and said, 'You know that the ones who are considered the rulers by the Gentiles show off their authority over them and their high-ranking officials order them around. But that's not the way it will be with you. Whoever wants to be great among you will be your servant. Whoever wants to be first among you will be the slave of all' " (Mark 10:42-44).

A poem found in Ecclesiastes 3 begins, "There's a season for everything and a time for every matter under the heavens" (Ecclesiastes 3:1). There is a time to "be still and know that I am God" (Psalm 46:10, KJV). There is a time to wait quietly and patiently. Our bodies, our minds, and our spirits need time for rest and reflection. But for most of us, most of the time, God gives us work to do while we wait patiently.

The spiritual practice suggested for this unit of lessons is to pray without ceasing. *Lectio Divina* is the practice of scriptural reading, meditation, and prayer intended to promote communion with God. The emphasis is on our devotion to God rather than on reading Scripture for greater knowledge. You might want to choose a verse, perhaps some phrases from this lesson's Key Verse to engage this practice this coming week: " 'Don't be afraid. . . . Your prayers have been heard.' "

Are you obediently responding to God's call on your life while you wait patiently and expectantly for God to act? How can the spiritual practice of Lectio Divina *help you wait patiently and faithfully for God to act?*

Dear God, thank you for the gift of Christmas, the coming of your Son and our Savior. Thank you for loving us, forgiving us, empowering us, and calling us to make a difference in your world. Help us to more deeply connect with you in this season of Advent; in Jesus' name we pray. Amen.

[1]From *Saturnalia*, by Macrobius (*tinyurl.com/3xycvckm*).
[2]From *Wonders of Wonders*, by Dietrich Bonhoeffer (Westminster John Knox Press, 2015).

The Spiritual Practice of Continuous Prayer

In Paul's first known letter to the church at Thessalonica, he concluded with specific instructions: "Rejoice always. Pray continually. Give thanks in every situation because this is God's will for you in Christ Jesus" (1 Thessalonians 5:16-18). So, how do we "pray continually"?

Brother Lawrence's classic book *The Practice of the Presence of God* had a profound influence on me. Brother Lawrence was born Nicholas Herman around 1610 in Herimenil, Lorraine, a duchy of France. He learned how to live with a near-constant awareness of God's presence in his life as he went about the rather menial tasks he was assigned in his monastery. As a cook, he carried on an almost constant conversation with God.

We can have this kind of relationship with God, too. We can talk to God as we go about our daily activities. One thing that helps me is to remember how extremely blessed I am and live with a constant attitude of gratitude. Perhaps my experiences will help you.

I begin my day by repeating my personal vow, which begins, "Dear God, today I will seek to love you with all my heart, soul, mind, and strength. I will express this love primarily by loving my neighbor and loving myself." It ends, "I will seek your will and wisdom, strive for detachment, work to develop more patience, practice your presence, and live in a state of gratitude."

I also like to pray what I call "arrow prayers." I may see a homeless person on the side of the road or a child playing outside. I pause for a moment and ask God's blessings and protection on that person. I have even used a pocket alarm to remind me each hour to connect with God. Use your creativity to discover what works for you to connect you to your Creator.

Think of one thing you can do this week to pray continually, and then plan to do it.

Focal Passage: Luke 1:26-38, 46-55
Background Text: Luke 1
Purpose Statement: To allow Mary's simple faith to inspire us

Luke 1:26-38, 46-55

26When Elizabeth was six months pregnant, God sent the angel Gabriel to Nazareth, a city in Galilee, 27to a virgin who was engaged to a man named Joseph, a descendant of David's house. The virgin's name was Mary. 28When the angel came to her, he said, "Rejoice, favored one! The Lord is with you!" 29She was confused by these words and wondered what kind of greeting this might be. 30The angel said, "Don't be afraid, Mary. God is honoring you. 31Look! You will conceive and give birth to a son, and you will name him Jesus. 32He will be great and he will be called the Son of the Most High. The Lord God will give him the throne of David his father. 33He will rule over Jacob's house forever, and there will be no end to his kingdom."

34Then Mary said to the angel, "How will this happen since I haven't had sexual relations with a man?"

35The angel replied, "The Holy Spirit will come over you and the power of the Most High will overshadow you. Therefore, the one who is to be born will be holy. He will be called God's Son. 36Look, even in her old age, your relative Elizabeth has conceived a son. This woman who was labeled 'unable to conceive' is now six months pregnant. ³⁷Nothing is impossible for God."

³⁸Then Mary said, "I am the Lord's servant. Let it be with me just as you have said." Then the angel left her. . . .

⁴⁶Mary said,

"With all my heart I glorify the Lord!
⁴⁷   In the depths of who I am I rejoice in God my savior.
⁴⁸ He has looked with favor on the low status of his servant.
    Look! From now on, everyone will consider me highly favored
⁴⁹   because the mighty one has done great things for me.
Holy is his name.
⁵⁰   He shows mercy to everyone,
        from one generation to the next,
        who honors him as God.
⁵¹He has shown strength with his arm.
    He has scattered those with arrogant thoughts and proud inclinations.
⁵²   He has pulled the powerful down from their thrones
        and lifted up the lowly.
⁵³He has filled the hungry with good things
    and sent the rich away empty-handed.
⁵⁴He has come to the aid of his servant Israel,
        remembering his mercy,
⁵⁵   just as he promised to our ancestors,
            to Abraham and to Abraham's descendants forever."

Key Verse: "Then Mary said, 'I am the Lord's servant. Let it be with me just as you have said.' Then the angel left her" (Luke 1:38).

Many years ago, I was struggling as a young adult. I was having difficulty trying to figure out what I was going to be "when I grew up." I had no direction in my life. I had dropped out of college and couldn't find a job I enjoyed and paid a living wage.

One day, my pious aunt told my mother I was simply out of God's will, though I felt this was not the case. She went on to explain that if God were pleased with me, then God would have bestowed greater blessings. In other words, she believed I had fallen out of favor with God.

In Luke's Gospel, we read that an angel said to Mary, "Do not be afraid, Mary, for you have found *favor* with God" (Luke 1:30, NRSV; italics added). The word rendered "favor" is the Greek word *charisma*, from the word *charis*. This word, which was commonly used in a greeting, means "that which creates joy." It was an announcement of God's blessings and approval. So what does it mean to find favor with God?

Our culture tells us material goods are a sign of God's favor, and Christians are often drawn into that way of thinking. Reading our text for this lesson should make it clear God has a different view, however. Jesus was not born into a rich family or a royal family, but rather to a poor peasant girl. Joseph was a manual worker. Mary found favor with God but had to endure a long, dangerous, exhausting journey while pregnant and had to give birth in unsanitary conditions with no family support. This woman, favored by God, would see her firstborn son arrested, humiliated, beaten, and killed on a cruel cross. God's idea of favor must be drastically different from what most people assume.

From beginning to end, Mary remained faithful to God. She must have been frightened when the angel first showed up to tell her what was about to take place. She must have feared for her son for many years. She surely was fearful for him when he was arrested. But through it all, her response was, "Let it be with me just as you have said" (verse 38).

As we reflect on this beautiful story, we can draw strength and encouragement from the simple but powerful faith of this poor young girl. Mary's example reminds us we can trust God to be faithful and to remain with us.

Jesus' Birth Foretold

As we saw in the previous lesson, Luke beautifully builds the anticipation of Jesus' birth by first relating the story of Zechariah, Elizabeth, and the announcement of John's birth. That text is a mirror-like reflection of the Annunciation story found in this text. The same angel came with essentially the same message. Of course, good comparative stories also need interesting contrast.

One story is about an elderly, married but childless couple; the other about a young unmarried woman. The older couple, no doubt, could hardly wait to announce their good news. For the young woman, being pregnant would have been a major scandal. One scene takes place in a grand Temple; the other in a tiny, simple home in a remote village.

Also, as noted in the previous lesson, Matthew's Gospel was originally intended to convince its readers Jesus was the long-expected Jewish Messiah. It begins with a genealogy of Jesus that traces him all the way back to Abraham and shows how he is descended from King David. This connection, of course, is a requirement for the Messiah.

Second Samuel 7:16 records God's promise to David that his descendants will always reign over Israel: "Your dynasty and your kingdom will be secured forever before me. Your throne will be established forever."

The various accounts of Jesus' birth include differences and therefore present challenges. While none of these should threaten our faith, and we can't address all of them here, we should note a couple of them.

First, Matthew's genealogy traces Jesus' lineage through Joseph, even though a few verses later, Matthew says Mary became pregnant by the Holy Spirit. Some people question why Matthew traced the genealogy of Jesus through Joseph if he was not Jesus' actual father.

Second, Jesus is recurrently referred to as the son of Joseph. Even Mary, admonishing Jesus after finding him in the Temple, said, "Your father and I have been worried. We've been looking for you!" (Luke 2:48). Another challenge for some people is the idea of the virgin birth because it is not mentioned anywhere else in Scripture.

While Luke wanted to convince his readers Jesus was the Savior of the world, not just the Jewish Messiah, he also wanted to confirm Jesus fulfilled Old Testament Scripture. Luke 1:27 tells us the angel Gabriel appeared "to a virgin who was engaged to a man named Joseph, a descendant of David's house. The virgin's name was Mary."

The Jews waited for many years for the coming of the Messiah. What can we learn from them as we wait for Jesus' return?

God's Promises

The angel Gabriel began with the greeting, "Rejoice, favored one! The Lord is with you!" (Luke 1:28). We might recall the words of Hannah, Samuel's mother, who had prayed for a child for so many years: "Let your servant find favor in your sight" (1 Samuel 1:18, NRSV). The angel then proclaimed to Mary, "The Lord is with you!" (Luke 1:28).

Matthew, relating the story from Joseph's perspective, wrote, "Now all of this took place so that what the Lord had spoken through the prophet would be fulfilled: Look! A virgin will become pregnant and give birth to a son, And they will call him, Emmanuel. (*Emmanuel* means 'God with us.')" (Matthew 1:22-23). This was seen as a fulfillment of Isaiah's prophecy: "Therefore, the Lord will give you a sign. The young woman is pregnant and is about to give birth to a son, and she will name him Immanuel" (Isaiah 7:14).

The idea of "God with us" has brought comfort to Christians through the ages. Especially during the COVID-19 pandemic, many have found comfort in this belief. It has always been tremendously encouraging to me that most of the call stories in Scripture include God's promise to be with the called one, to bless and protect.

When God called Abraham, God immediately promised, "I will make of you a great nation and will bless you" (Genesis 12:2). When God called Moses, he asked, "Who am I to go to Pharaoh and to bring the Israelites out of Egypt?" God immediately responded, "I'll be with you" (Exodus 3:11-12). In 1 Samuel 3, we read about Hannah and her son, Samuel, whom she dedicated to God. In 1 Samuel 3:19, we read, "So Samuel grew up, and the LORD was with him, not allowing any of his words to fail."

God promised Isaiah not only personal protection, but protection for "Israel my servant": "Don't fear, because I am with you; don't be afraid, for I am your God. I will strengthen you, I will surely help you; I will hold you with my righteous strong hand" (Isaiah 41:10). God called Jeremiah and said, "They will attack you, but they won't defeat you, because I am with you and will rescue you" (Jeremiah 1:19).

When Jesus gave his disciples what became known as the Great Commission, he included the promise, "I myself will be with you every day until the end of this present age" (Matthew 28:20).

Like her spiritual ancestors, Mary received and believed God's promise to be with her, even in this confusing and unprecedented time.

Do you feel God is always with you? Is there anything you might need to do to become more aware of God's presence?

Experiencing God

Some Bible scholars have suggested Mary's visit by the angel reveals four stages of a spiritual experience.[1] The first stage is fear. Mary was apparently frightened by the angel's presence. Mary was surely not the only one who has been overwhelmed when encountering the presence and power of the living God. We saw in the previous lesson that Zechariah was overcome with fear.

The second stage is perplexity. Our text tells us Mary was "confused" (Luke 1:29). She said to the angel, "How can this be, since I am a virgin?" (verse 34, NRSV). When the initial shock and awe of our encounter with God starts to fade, we make an attempt at understanding what is going on and what God is doing.

The third stage is to recognize all things are possible with God. In God's presence, we recognize divine power in contrast with human inadequacy. This leads to the final stage, which is an obedient response, a personal commitment that grows out of the realization God is indeed in control. Mary believed the angel when he said, "Nothing is impossible for God" (verse 37), and responded, "Let it be with me just as you have said" (verse 38).

At the beginning of my pastoral ministry, I had a dream that had a great influence on my life. My wife and I had checked into a downtown hotel in Greenville, Mississippi. We were there to attend my first Methodist annual conference as a newly appointed pastor.

Early the next morning as I was lying in bed, half asleep but half awake in a somewhat meditative state, I had what I consider a spiritual vision. I'm not a mystic, and I'm always skeptical of stories about mystical experiences. Many, I'm sure, would simply say I fell back asleep and had a dream. If so, it would be the most real dream I'm ever experienced.

In this vision or dream, I found myself in heaven, standing in a great hallway. In front of me were beautiful giant doors. Somehow I knew I was about to be called in to stand before God and to give an account for how I had lived my life.

In that moment, I experienced a deep emotion I had never felt before and have never felt since. I had no fear of punishment, but rather of God's disappointment. In that moment, I recognized as never before just how richly God had blessed me.

I had been a moral person and had trusted God to save me from eternal damnation. However, I realized I could have done so much more to pay it forward. There were so many times I had fallen short, missed the mark. I had been good while God had wanted me to be "good for something." I had been a lukewarm follower of Jesus while he had been calling me to a total commitment of my life.

I wished with every fiber of my being I could have another chance to commit my life completely and totally to God, to be a blessing to others as God had blessed me. And, suddenly, I found myself back in the hotel room.

I sensed God's voice saying, "You've got it! I'm giving you another chance to serve me, to make a difference, to pay it forward, to use my blessings to bless others."

Over the years when I have become discouraged, I remember that morning in Greenville, Mississippi. When I wonder what difference I am making, when I come under attack, or when no one seems to appreciate my sacrifices, I remember that morning. It was a great gift. Whether it was a dream, a vision, or even a figment of my imagination, it was a gift that has encouraged me, motivated me, and deepened my faith for over 30 years.

Throughout her life, Mary no doubt returned in her mind to that visit from the angel and recalled his words to her: "Nothing is impossible for God" (verse 37). And she reaffirmed her commitment to the will of God: "I am the Lord's servant. Let it be with me just as you have said" (verse 38).

What experiences have you had with God? What stages did you move through during these experiences?

Our Response

Take a moment and try to imagine what it must have been like for Mary. She was a young, poor, uneducated woman living in a remote village, with no reason to believe her life would be exceptional in any way.

Our text tells us she was engaged to Joseph. The Greek word rendered "engaged" by the translators of the CEB is *mnesteuo*. The New International Version says Mary was "pledged to be married to a man named Joseph." The Revised Standard Version reads, "To a virgin betrothed to a man whose name was Joseph."

This period of engagement usually lasted a year and was considered as binding as the formal marriage. The engagement could be broken only by divorce.

Can you imagine how her family and friends must have responded when she tried to tell them about this encounter with the angel Gabriel? "Oh, you are pregnant, but you haven't been with a man? Yes, I see. Sure."

"It was the Holy Spirit that got you pregnant. Wow! That must have really been something!"

It's hard for me to believe Mary wasn't condemned by many and laughed at by others. But she kept her faith in God and remained faithful. Despite the scorn, the difficulties, and the heartache that came to her, she remained true to her initial commitment: "Let it be with me just as you have said" (Luke 1:38).

Key to remaining faithful and true to our commitment to God is prayer. The idea of "praying without ceasing" may seem daunting, but practicing it makes it less so. Allow Mary's faithfulness and commitment to God to encourage you to infuse every part of every day with prayer so you, too, can respond to God, "Let it be with me just as you have said."

How have you responded when you were condemned or ridiculed, even though you knew you were innocent? Have you remained faithful even when others laughed at you or scorned you for doing the right thing?

Dear God, help us increase our awareness of your constant presence in our lives and to be inspired by the amazing faithfulness of Jesus' mother, Mary; in Jesus' name we pray. Amen.

¹From *The Interpreter's Bible*, Volume 8; pages 37-38.

Focal Passage: Luke 2:25-38
Background Text: Luke 2
Purpose Statement: To remember God rewards those who act faithfully

Luke 2:25-38

25 **A man named Simeon was in Jerusalem. He was righteous and devout. He eagerly anticipated the restoration of Israel, and the Holy Spirit rested on him.** **26** **The Holy Spirit revealed to him that he wouldn't die before he had seen the Lord's Christ.** **27** **Led by the Spirit, he went into the temple area. Meanwhile, Jesus' parents brought the child to the temple so that they could do what was customary under the Law.** **28** **Simeon took Jesus in his arms and praised God. He said,**

29 **"Now, master, let your servant go in peace according to your word,**

30   **because my eyes have seen your salvation.**
31 **You prepared this salvation in the presence of all peoples.**

32 **It's a light for revelation to the Gentiles**
    and a glory for your people Israel."

33 **His father and mother were amazed by what was said about him.** **34** **Simeon blessed them and said to Mary his mother, "This boy is assigned to be the cause of the**

falling and rising of many in Israel and to be a sign that generates opposition ³⁵so that the inner thoughts of many will be revealed. And a sword will pierce your innermost being too."

³⁶There was also a prophet, Anna the daughter of Phanuel, who belonged to the tribe of Asher. She was very old. After she married, she lived with her husband for seven years. ³⁷She was now an 84-year-old widow. She never left the temple area but worshipped God with fasting and prayer night and day. ³⁸She approached at that very moment and began to praise God and to speak about Jesus to everyone who was looking forward to the redemption of Jerusalem.

Key Verse: "A man named Simeon was in Jerusalem. He was righteous and devout. He eagerly anticipated the restoration of Israel, and the Holy Spirit rested on him" (Luke 2:25).

Perhaps you have seen the 2007 movie *The Bucket List*, starring Jack Nicholson and Morgan Freeman. The story is about two terminally-ill men who set out on a road trip to accomplish the list of things they hope to achieve before they die (or "kick the bucket," as some people say). Many of us have such a list.

I had bypass heart surgery over 20 years ago at the age of 47. The doctors told me it was a miracle I had not had a heart attack. Moreover, had that happened, I would not have survived. Coming so close to death, especially at such an early age, led me to develop "bucket list" thinking. I decided I was not going to wait until I retired to travel as I had always planned. This has led me to visit over 35 countries and to complete two pastor exchanges in England. I have been to all 50 states except Hawaii.

I also included on my list certain other goals. My wife and I love to hike, especially in the mountains. This past year, I finally hiked to the top of Mount LeConte and back down in one day. This was a 20-mile hike in my favorite hiking spot, the Great Smoky Mountains National Park.

This past December, eight days before I turned 71, I ran my first marathon. In addition to these fun things (well, perhaps the marathon wasn't exactly fun), I've also had some serious things on my list. It is balanced with professional and spiritual goals.

In the text for this lesson, we read about two people who had amazing dreams. Apparently, they had only one thing on their bucket lists.

Confirmation and Hope

I love Luke's stories about Simeon and Anna, who simply wanted to see the Messiah before they died. Luke doesn't tell us exactly why this was so important to them. Were they primarily interested in the political ramifications? The Jews expected the Messiah to drive out the hated Romans and to restore the Davidic kingdom. Perhaps they wanted their faith in God confirmed in a dramatic fashion: to know what they had always been taught and believed was true, to know God is real, and to confirm God is faithful.

People can fall prey to doubt and distrust quite easily over time, especially when their religion is primarily based on holding to the right doctrines. Practitioners of many faiths think their teachings are nearer the ultimate truth than others. How can we know for sure ours is the right one? Wouldn't most of us, perhaps all of us, love to see some manifestation of God's power that convincingly confirms our own beliefs?

While confirmation of their faith and affirmation of Simeon's and Anna's life commitments may have been the basis of their deep-seated desire to see the Messiah before they died, our text suggests this was not likely their motivation. Luke tells us Simeon "was righteous and devout" and "the Holy Spirit rested on him" (Luke 2:25). Furthermore, "the Holy Spirit revealed to him that he wouldn't die before he had seen the Lord's Christ" (verse 26). Anna was so deeply committed to God, she "worshipped God with fasting and prayer night and day" (verse 37).

Perhaps Simeon and Anna had lived long enough and seen enough to lose hope in any earthly alternative to a radical new source of salvation. Perhaps they had lost faith in their political and religious leaders.

While most Jews still longed for the day God would break into reality by some miraculous means, overthrow Israel's overlords, and change the trajectory of history, perhaps Simeon and Anna were happy living a quiet life of prayer and watchful obedience. Perhaps they had no dreams of a military coup or political upheaval, but of God's work in broken lives, cynical minds, and the spiritually hungry.

We can never know for sure. Scripture doesn't tell us. Perhaps Simeon and Anna were motivated by "all of the above."

Who or what confirms your faith? What motivates you to hold on to hope when circumstances seem to suggest you should give up?

Salvation for All

We have already seen how the author of Luke wanted to convince his readers Jesus was not only the long-awaited Jewish Messiah, but actually the Savior of the world. This is nowhere in the book more clearly stated than in the text for this lesson. Luke tells us Simeon took Jesus into his arms and announced, "You prepared this salvation in the presence of all people. It's a light for revelation to the Gentiles and a glory for your people Israel" (Luke 2:31-32).

Nothing the apostle Paul said or did had a greater influence on the early church than his insistence that the gospel was intended for the Jews and the Gentiles. The first thing Paul wrote in his letter to the church at Rome, after what serves as his introduction, makes his belief about this clear: "That's why I'm ready to preach the gospel also to you who are in Rome. I'm not ashamed of the gospel: it is God's own power for salvation to all who have faith in God, to the Jew first and also to the Greek" (Romans 1:15-16).

Luke sought to convince his readers this was indeed Jesus' intention, not just Paul's opinion. In our text, Luke reveals the universal nature of the gospel, good news for the Gentiles as well as the people of Israel. But this was not the first time Luke insisted on this truth, and it is not the last in his Gospel. Earlier in the chapter, we read where the angel brought good news to the shepherds: "Wonderful, joyous news for *all* people" (Luke 2:10; italics added).

In the third chapter, Luke introduces the preaching of Zechariah and Elizabeth's son, John, and quoted Isaiah 40:4-5: "A voice crying out in the wilderness; 'Prepare the way for the LORD; make his paths straight. Every valley will be filled, and every mountain and hill will be leveled. The crooked will be made straight and the rough places made smooth. All humanity will see God's salvation'" (Luke 3:4-6).

Throughout his Gospel, Luke indicates God is particularly interested in offering salvation to all people. You may recall this Gospel is the first volume of a two-volume work that also includes the Acts of the Apostles.

When Jesus appeared to the disciples at the end of Luke, "he said to them, 'This is what is written: the Christ will suffer and rise from the dead on the third day, and a change of heart and life for the forgiveness of sins must be preached in his name to *all* nations, beginning from Jerusalem'" (Luke 24:46-47; italics added). At the beginning of Acts, Luke reports that the risen Jesus appeared to his disciples and said, "You will receive power when the Holy Spirit has come upon you, and you will be my witnesses in Jerusalem, in all Judea and Samaria, and to the end of the earth" (Acts 1:8).

At the end of Acts, Luke reports Paul met with the Jewish leaders in Rome. Most refused to believe what the apostle told them about Jesus. In response, he quoted Isaiah 6:9-10. This passage suggests the ancient Israelites refused to hear the truth: *"This people's senses have become calloused, and they've become hard of hearing, and they've shut their eyes"* (Acts 28:27). Paul concluded the meeting by saying, "Therefore, be certain of this: God's salvation has been sent to the Gentiles. They will listen!" (Acts 28:28).

Luke not only sought to convince his readers the divine gift of salvation was for Jews and Gentiles, he also sought to stress God's love for the poor and disenfranchised. More than in any other Gospel, Jesus reached out to this group, including women, tax collectors, the disabled, and social outcasts. More than anyone else, Luke mentioned Jesus associating with sinners. Those thus identified were often poor commoners who were shunned by the Pharisees and Sadducees.

Even the hated Samaritans get good press in Luke's Gospel. Luke is the only one who included the story of the good Samaritan. No one else related the story of the ten lepers when only the Samaritan returned to thank Jesus. The occasion when Jesus rejected the idea of calling down fire on a Samaritan village is found only in Luke.

One of the real surprises in this amazing Gospel is the important place women take in the narrative. This often comes in the form of couples. We have already experienced this in the first three lessons of this unit.

Our texts have recounted the stories of Zechariah and Elizabeth, Joseph and Mary, and Simeon and Anna. There are numerous other accounts of Jesus' association with women in a significant role. For example, Luke is the only book to tell us there were women who traveled with Jesus "through the cities and villages, preaching and proclaiming the good news of God's kingdom" (Luke 8:1).

Anna's inclusion in Luke's Gospel account is intentional. At the outset, Luke was careful to make note of women who encountered Jesus. Her years of patient service and constant vigilance had paid off. "She approached at that very moment and began to praise God and to speak about Jesus to everyone who was looking forward to the redemption of Jerusalem" (2:38).

Think about your life of faith, your walk with Christ. What have you had to wait for? What has come slowly for you? What did the act of waiting teach you?

Challenging the Ways of the World

Most of us prefer to talk about God's divine love, mercy, and grace; but Luke reminds us God's kingdom will always stand in stark contrast to the material world we see all around us. "This boy is assigned to be the cause of the falling and rising of many in Israel and to be a sign that generates opposition," Simeon said to Mary (Luke 2:34).

The great fourth-century theologian Augustine addressed this reality by using the illustration of two cities. The City of Man is characterized by those who love self. The City of God is filled by those who love God. Those in the material city are prideful and ambitious. Those in the heavenly city love their neighbor and seek to bring honor and glory to God.

Jesus came into the world to clarify God's commission. God promised to bless Abraham and called him and his descendants to be a blessing to "*all* the families of the earth" (Genesis 12:3; italics added). But the Jews misinterpreted this calling and wanted to claim his blessings only for themselves. Jesus, on the other hand, insisted God's will is for us to love all others, even our enemies. Just as God's instructions to Abraham indicated, we are to use our divine blessings to bless others.

The world, of course, rejects this attitude. It teaches we should look out for ourselves. The 1987 move *Wall Street* clearly illustrates this mindset. Michael Douglas plays Gordon Gekko, a wealthy, unscrupulous corporate raider, who says, "Greed, for lack of a better word, is good. Greed is right. Greed works. [It] captures the essence of the evolutionary spirit. Greed, in all of its forms; greed for life, for money, for love, knowledge—has marked the upward surge of mankind."[1] Unfortunately, while never stating it so bluntly, some Christians have adopted this philosophy, too.

Luke wanted the world to know Jesus and wanted the world to understand God's kingdom is not compatible with a materialistic culture. God's kingdom doesn't put profits before people or rules and religious rituals before the genuine needs of our neighbors.

The current situation in which I find myself has been a real lesson in regard to this reality. As I write this, I am experiencing great emotional pain. It's been reported that in the last 24 hours thousands of people have died nationwide from COVID-19. I mourn the deaths of so many. However, what is also troubling to me is the attitude of some people who have said the stay-at-home orders are destroying our economy.

Apparently, many people believe supporting our economy, among other concerns, is more important than a few thousand lives. After all, their argument goes, more people die from the flu, cancer, heart disease, and other ailments than have died from COVID-19. One well-known political pundit even insisted many of those who died "were on their last legs anyway."

In what ways does our culture challenge your practice of the Christian faith? In what ways does your practice of the Christian faith challenge our culture?

The Power of Hope and Rewards of Righteousness

When we read our text for this lesson, we can see the power of hope. Here is a man who year after year anticipated the restoration of Israel. Here is an 84-year-old woman who day after day, night after night, month after month, year after year never gave up hope. What, we may ask, kept these two going? Apparently, they were extremely intentional about their relationship with God. James 4:7-8 reads, "Therefore, submit to God. Resist the devil, and he will run away from you. Come near to God, and he will come near to you."

Simeon and Anna remained hopeful, no doubt because they believed God is faithful. This faith that God would keep promises in the future must surely have been based on their life experiences. They must have repeatedly found God faithful in many ways, or they would have given up long before their encounter with Jesus in the Temple.

They were rewarded for their faithfulness. Hebrews 11:6 tells us God "rewards those who earnestly seek him" (NRSV). Life doesn't always work out just the way we want, not even for those who love God. Jesus admitted God "makes the sun rise on both the evil and the good and sends rain on both the righteous and the unrighteous" (Matthew 5:45). But God has promised to be with the faithful, to ultimately protect and bless us.

As I sit and write this, it's actually Good Friday. I'm reminded of Tony Campolo's Good Friday sermon, "It's Friday. . . . But Sunday's Comin!" This text and the examples of Simeon and Anna remind us that things may take longer than we wish, and they may not look exactly the way we might like, but God is faithful. And God rewards our faithfulness.

As you seek this week to pray without ceasing, remember at least part of what this means is to be as constantly aware as possible that God is with you at all times. God is always ready and eager to connect with us. This week, try to stay connected. When you see something beautiful in nature, let it remind you of God's creative power, and express your gratitude. When you see a need, ask God to fill that need and to use you to do it if possible.

What are you currently waiting for? What gives you hope and assurance as you wait?

Great and loving God, give us a keen awareness of your presence in our lives, and help us better connect with you; in Jesus' name we pray. Amen.

[1]From *imdb.com/title/tt0094291/characters/nm0000140*.

Focal Passage: Revelation 3:20–4:11
Background Text: Same
Purpose Statement: To more fully appreciate the radical nature of God's patient love

Revelation 3:20–4:11

²⁰Look! I'm standing at the door and knocking. If any hear my voice and open the door, I will come in to be with them, and will have dinner with them, and they will have dinner with me. ²¹As for those who emerge victorious, I will allow them to sit with me on my throne, just as I emerged victorious and sat down with my Father on his throne. ²²If you can hear, listen to what the Spirit is saying to the churches."

¹After this I looked and there was a door that had been opened in heaven. The first voice that I had heard, which sounded like a trumpet, said to me, "Come up here, and I will show you what must take place after this." ²At once I was in a Spirit-inspired trance and I saw a throne in heaven, and someone was seated on the throne. ³The one seated there looked like jasper and carnelian, and surrounding the throne was a rainbow that looked like an emerald. ⁴Twenty-four thrones, with twenty-four elders seated upon them, surrounded the throne. The elders were dressed in white clothing and had gold crowns on their heads. ⁵From the throne came lightning, voices, and thunder. In front of the

throne were seven flaming torches, which are the seven spirits of God. [6]Something like a glass sea, like crystal, was in front of the throne.

In the center, by the throne, were four living creatures encircling the throne. These creatures were covered with eyes on the front and on the back. [7]The first living creature was like a lion. The second living creature was like an ox. The third living creature had a face like a human being. And the fourth living creature was like an eagle in flight. [8]Each of the four living creatures had six wings, and each was covered all around and on the inside with eyes. They never rest day or night, but keep on saying,

"Holy, holy, holy is the Lord God Almighty,
    who was and is and is coming."

[9]Whenever the living creatures give glory, honor, and thanks to the one seated on the throne, who lives forever and always, [10]the twenty-four elders fall before the one seated on the throne. They worship the one who lives forever and always. They throw down their crowns before the throne and say,

[11]"You are worthy, our Lord and God,
    to receive glory and honor and power,
        because you created all things.
    It is by your will that they existed and were created."

Key Verse: "Look! I'm standing at the door and knocking. If any hear my voice and open the door, I will come in to be with them, and will have dinner with them, and they will have dinner with me" (Revelation 3:20).

Many Christians make pilgrimages to Israel to visit the places "where Jesus walked." I encourage every Christian who is able to make this trip, as well as to travel to Turkey and visit the biblical sites found there. The most popular Christian tours in this region are the "Footsteps of Paul" and "Churches of Revelation." My favorite archaeological sites there are Ephesus and Laodicea.

While visited by far fewer tourists and pilgrims than Ephesus, the ruins of Laodicea are quite impressive. The site includes a bath house, a magnificent aqueduct, and two theaters. One of the neat things is this site is still being excavated, so visitors often get a chance to see archaeologists at work.

Laodicea was an important, wealthy city in New Testament times. It was located on the major trade route between Ephesus and Syria and was well-known for its banking and textile production.

While not all scholars agree, most have traditionally dated the writing of Revelation during the reign of the Roman emperor Domitian (AD 81–96). He was infamous for being the first Roman emperor who declared himself a god while still alive. He severely persecuted and killed those who refused to worship him. This demand placed Christians living in Laodicea in a difficult position. Their participation in widespread trade made them especially vulnerable, and their wealth was certainly at stake.

Under these extreme circumstances, many in Laodicea chose to compromise their faith. Of the seven churches addressed in the Book of Revelation, the one at Laodicea is the only one about which the author had absolutely nothing good to say.

God's assessment was severe: "I know your works. You are neither cold nor hot. I wish that you were either cold or hot. So because you are lukewarm, and neither hot nor cold, I'm about to spit you out of my mouth. After all, you say, 'I'm rich, and I've grown wealthy, and I don't need a thing.' You don't realize that you are miserable, pathetic, poor, blind, and naked" (Revelation 3:15-17).

John probably used the lukewarm metaphor because the water for the city of Laodicea came from six miles away by aqueduct. It was neither hot like the hot springs of Hierapolis a few miles to the north, nor cold like the water from a spring or a well. But God had not given up on the Christians in Laodicea. True to the divine nature, God remained patient, showing steadfast love, waiting for them to "change [their] hearts and lives" (verse 19).

We might wonder whether the church in North America needs to pay close attention to Revelation's message to the church at Laodicea. Are we sometimes guilty of having a tepid, halfhearted, unenthusiastic faith? Have we become so materially comfortable we don't feel the need for a meaningful life transformation and relationship with God?

Just as God had not given up on the Laodicean Christians, God has not given up on us. God has placed in the heart of each person a God-sized hole, the spiritual need for a relationship with God. People may try to meet this need temporarily through pleasures they enjoy. Some use material things as a way to satisfy this need: a new suit or dress, a new car or boat. However, these things satisfy for only a short time. Then we have to find something else to fill the hole in our hearts. According to the author of Revelation, God has a better idea, and God waits patiently for us to respond.

A Different Kind of Book

To understand the text for this lesson, we need to understand the wider context. The Book of Revelation is not an easy book to read. It is apocalyptic literature, the word *apocalypse* here meaning "revelation." Generally, it can mean any revelation or prophecy but is more often used to describe a type of Jewish or Christian literature written during the period between the Old Testament and the New Testament and on into the time of the early Christian church. This was a time of great messianic expectation on the part of the Jews and messianic fulfillment for Christians.

Apocalyptic literature usually had to do with God's final purpose and typically described a cataclysmic encounter between the forces of good and the forces of evil. This concern with eschatological issues—that is, interest in death, divine judgment, and end times—is in major contrast with Old Testament prophecies that were generally more concerned with present realities. In fact, many modern scholars believe Jews did not traditionally believe in an afterlife until the Babylonian exile in the sixth century BC.

The Book of Daniel is perhaps the closest example of this type of literature found in the Old Testament and is considered by many to be a prototype. Apocalyptic literature was often composed during times of persecution in something like secret code to address the fears of those being persecuted and to give them some hope for the future. These writings are extremely allegorical and symbolic by design and not meant to be taken literally.

For example, the immediate concern of the author of Revelation was the persecution of the early church. The beast mentioned in Revelation 13 almost surely should be understood as the Roman emperor. Basically, the message was that, while it may look like your persecutors are winning, God is in control. God will ultimately take care of you because Jesus has already won the ultimate victory.

The early Christians believed they would see the end of this present evil age and experience God's new kingdom on earth. No book expresses this hope in more powerful and vivid language than the Book of Revelation. This is articulated most explicitly in Revelation 21:1-4.

How do you respond to reading from the Book of Revelation? Do you draw strength, encouragement, and hope from it?

Warnings and Encouragement

After the introduction in Revelation 1, John recorded a series of letters to the persecuted Christians living in the western portion of Asia Minor, where the author had been exiled because of his refusal to worship the emperor. The letters were originally for the churches at Ephesus, Smyrna, Pergamum, Thyatira, Sardis, Philadelphia, and Laodicea.

In these letters, the author encouraged the Christians to remain faithful in spite of the persecution. He even insisted they should have no fear of death because in God's new kingdom, "death will be no more" (Revelation 21:4).

This, of course, supports the teaching of the apostle Paul, who wrote to the church at Corinth, "Death has been swallowed up by a victory. Where is your victory, Death? Where is your sting, Death? . . . Thanks be to God, who gives us this victory through our Lord Jesus Christ!" (1 Corinthians 15:54-55, 57).

Throughout the letters to the seven churches, John recorded the terrible things that would come upon them if they didn't "wake up" and the many rewards awaiting the Christians who remained loyal to Jesus Christ and refused to worship the Roman emperors as divine. "As for those who emerge victorious," God promised, "I will allow them to sit with me on my throne, just as I emerged victorious and sat down with my Father on his throne. If you can hear, listen to what the Spirit is saying to the churches" (Revelation 3:21-22).

What motivates you the most: the warnings regarding punishments or the promises of rewards? Do you need both? something else?

Standing at the Door

Having decided to enjoy the financial benefits of obedience to the emperor over faithfully following Christ, the Christians at Laodicea found themselves materially wealthy but spiritually poor.

In 1975, a reporter conducted a now-famous interview with Mother Teresa. In that interview, the Nobel Peace Prize winner insisted the spiritual poverty of the Western world is much greater than the physical poverty of the ones she served in India. She explained that millions of people in America suffer tremendous loneliness and emptiness and feel unloved and unwanted. Their money doesn't satisfy, but they don't know what will. What they are missing, Mother Teresa proclaimed, is a "living relationship with God."[1]

This is what John insisted God wanted to offer the people of Laodicea through Jesus Christ. "Look! I'm standing at the door and knocking. If any hear my voice and open the door, I will come in to be with them, and will have dinner with them, and they will have dinner with me" (Revelation 3:20). For this response, God patiently waited for them, and God waits for us, to open the door.

The verses that follow in Chapter 4 describe John's vision of God's throne, where God promised "those who emerge victorious" will also sit (verse 21). What a promise!

John saw an open door and heard a voice that "sounded like a trumpet" (4:1). He was "in a Spirit-inspired trance" (verse 2; "in the spirit," NRSV), and looking into heaven, saw a throne where someone was seated. John then described the one on the throne and all that surrounded the throne: a rainbow; 24 elders dressed in white and wearing gold crowns; lightning, voices, and thunder coming from the throne; "seven flaming torches" and "something like a glass sea, like crystal" (verses 2-6).

He described four living creatures around the throne who "never rest day or night, but keep on saying, 'Holy, holy, holy is the Lord God Almighty, who was and is and is coming'" (verse 8). Their unending chorus prompted the 24 elders to "throw down their crowns before the throne and say, 'You are worthy, our Lord and God, to receive glory and honor and power, because you created all things. It is by your will that they existed and were created'" (verses 10-11).

Like the Christians at Laodicea, we are invited to join this heavenly worship service. But also like them, we must choose to put our relationship with God above all other relationships and loyalties. We must choose to open the door.

During the four weeks of Advent, we have anticipated the coming of the Christ Child. But we have also spent time reflecting on our anticipation of his second coming. The church has been waiting for over 2,000 years, but this text reminds us Jesus stands at the door of each heart, patiently waiting, every day. He knocks because he wants us to invite him in.

As you continue to practice consistent prayer, schedule your time with God each day. Perhaps you might set as a goal to pause at least five times a day and seek to connect with God. Remember God's faithfulness and patient love toward us, and commit to spend time in prayer with God and Jesus, who stands at the door.

What is your response to the one standing at the door of your heart? Are there times or situations in which you refuse to let him in? What does God's patience with you reveal about God? What can we learn and apply from God's radical, patient love?

Loving God, thank you for your presence in our lives and your desire to live in our hearts and minds. Help us deepen our relationship with you, to hear your call upon our lives, to learn of your ways, and to do your will; in Jesus' name we pray. Amen.

[1]From *https://patch.com/california/lakeforest-ca/bp--the-day-mother-teresa-told-me-your-poverty-is-gree85a671097*

Daily Bible Readings (Unit 2)

December 27
Genesis 1:9-13

December 28
Job 12:7-10

December 29
Luke 12:22-28

December 30
Isaiah 40:6-8

December 31
Isaiah 40:12-17

January 1
Isaiah 40:21-26

January 2
Psalm 19:1-6

January 3
Genesis 3:6-8

January 4
Jeremiah 23:23-24

January 5
Psalm 34:17-19

January 6
Psalm 16:7-11

January 7
Matthew 5:8

January 8
Genesis 28:10-17

January 9
Isaiah 6:1-13

January 10
Luke 15: 8-10

January 11
Daniel 10:5-9

January 12
Revelation 4:1-11

January 13
Revelation 6:12-17

January 14
Micah 6:6-8

January 15
Acts 16:25-31

January 16
Mark 9:2-8

January 17
John 1:14, 16-18

January 18
Habakkuk 3:2-4

January 19
Deuteronomy
5:23-27

January 20
Ezekiel 1:26-28

January 21
2 Corinthians 4:1-6

January 22
Numbers 6:22-27

January 23
Exodus 24:29-35

January 24
Psalm 150:1-6

January 25
Ephesians 5:19-20

January 26
Psalm 98:1-9

January 27
Luke 2:8- 20

January 28
Psalm 95:1-5

January 29
Revelation 5:6-10

January 30
Revelation 19:1-10

Unit 2
Wonder

In this five-lesson unit, we explore various ways human beings have experienced God's sublime glory, filling them with awe and wonder. We are a busy people rushing from place to place and task to task as the hands of the clock chase each other around the dial. We get caught up in the mundane reality of ordinary life, and if we do not stop, we can so easily miss the extraordinary and sublime experience of entering into God's presence. These lessons call us to slow down, observe, and experience God in our midst.

In Lesson 5, we examine Psalm 19 and consider how God is powerfully and profoundly revealed by the beauty of creation that surrounds us. It begins, "Heaven is declaring God's glory; the sky is proclaiming his handiwork" (Psalm 19:1).

The text for Lesson 6 is from Isaiah 6, where we read about Isaiah's call to be a spokesman for God and reflect on our own divine call. At the beginning of the prophet's holy encounter, the winged creatures shouted, "Holy, holy, holy is the LORD of heavenly forces! All the earth is filled with God's glory!" (Isaiah 6:3).

Lesson 7 leads us to explore Mark's version of the story of Jesus' Transfiguration. This narrative, along with the others in this unit, is a valuable reminder that an encounter with God can change our lives forever.

Few people have likely had the relationship with God that Moses had. Lesson 8 encourages us to think about our own relationship with God, how carefully we listen, and how faithfully we obey.

Finally, in Lesson 9, we will once again examine a passage from the Book of Revelation. This lesson encourages us to continually offer praise and adoration to the God of all creation. Only God is worthy of our worship.

50 Adult Bible Studies

Focal Passage: Psalm 19:1-6
Background Text: Psalm 19
Purpose Statement: To affirm God as the Creator and Sustainer of everything

Psalm 19:1-6

¹Heaven is declaring God's glory;
   the sky is proclaiming his handiwork.
²One day gushes the news to the next,
      and one night informs another what needs to be known.
³Of course, there's no speech, no words—
         their voices can't be heard—
⁴   but their sound extends throughout the world;
         their words reach the ends of the earth.
God has made a tent in heaven for the sun.
⁵The sun is like a groom
      coming out of his honeymoon suite;
      like a warrior, it thrills at running its course.
⁶It rises in one end of the sky;
      its circuit is complete at the other.
         Nothing escapes its heat.

Key Verse: "Heaven is declaring God's glory; the sky is proclaiming his handiwork" (Psalm 19:1).

   In the sixth century BC, the ancient Israelites found themselves in captivity in Babylon, where they faced a major dilemma. Should they continue to worship Yahweh, or begin to worship the whole pantheon of Mesopotamian gods, including Marduk, the patron deity of the city of Babylon? Even the Israelites who worshiped Yahweh had generally believed Yahweh was the God of Israel, not the universal, one and only God of the universe. Moreover, most people at the time, including most Israelites, believed the army with the most powerful god or gods won the battles, and Babylon had indeed conquered Judah and pretty much destroyed Jerusalem.

We can see this dilemma voiced in Psalm 137: "Alongside Babylon's streams, there we sat down, crying because we remembered Zion. We hung our lyres up in the trees there because that's where our captors asked us to sing; our tormentors requested songs of joy: 'Sing us a song about Zion!' they said. But how could we possibly sing the LORD's song on foreign soil?" (Psalm 137:1-4).

In the midst of their pain and hardships in captivity, the religious leaders began work to renew the Jewish faith. They came to believe Yahweh had allowed them to be conquered by the Babylonians as a punishment for their sin. They came to understand Yahweh was not only the God of Israel, but rather the one and only God, Creator and Sustainer of the universe. The challenge was to make sure they never again were so disobedient that God would allow something like captivity to happen.

If they were going to make sure they never again so flagrantly broke God's laws and failed to do God's will, they needed to have a clear understanding of what those laws were. To address this problem, the priests began to compile what became much of what we call the Old Testament. That document began, "In the beginning God created the heaven and the earth" (Genesis 1:1, KJV). This was an affirmation that the God the Israelites worshiped was indeed the one and only God of all creation, including Babylon.

Can you imagine how important this belief became to the Israelites living in captivity? They must have felt a great deal of encouragement and hope, especially when they remembered Yahweh's prophets had predicted their captivity would happen if they didn't turn from their sin.

Now what they needed to do was ask God's forgiveness and return to faithful obedience. If God is the Creator and Sustainer of the universe, God can surely keep promises to watch over us and care for us, even in the midst of captivity or a pandemic.

Of course, we are always living in the midst of captivity and pandemics of one sort or another, aren't we? We are captive to our materialistic culture, to our personal prejudices, to our addictions. There are always diseases of the body, mind, and spirit. Our daily existence is filled with the stresses of life that bring anxiety and fear. We all have our bad habits, hurts, and hangups.

Like Psalm 19, the old hymn "Never Alone" reminds us God is the Creator and Sustainer of everything. God is in control of our world and has promised never to forsake us.

An Anthology of Hebrew Religious Poetry

The Psalms of our Old Testament were first the book of hymns and the prayer book of the ancient Jews. Perhaps we might more accurately call the Psalms their anthology of religious poetry. An anthology is simply a collection of poems or writing, and the Book of Psalms is a wonderful, rich collection including many hymns of praise and thanksgiving.

The Bible is, of course, a collection of smaller books written over many hundreds of years. What we Christians call the Old Testament is, in reality, the Hebrew Bible. Jews call this collection of books the *Tanak*, also spelled *tanakh*. This name is actually an acronym that comes from the way the Jews divide the book. The Torah is the book of Law, which is made up of the first five books.

The second division of the Tanak is the *Nevi'im*, the book of prophets. The *Nevi'im* are divided into two groups. The Former Prophets consist of the narrative books of Joshua, Judges, Samuel, and Kings, while the Latter Prophets include the books of Isaiah, Jeremiah, Ezekiel, and the Twelve Minor Prophets.

The third and last section of the Hebrew Bible to be written is the *Kethuvim*, that is "the writings." While most Jews consider these books to have been divinely inspired, they don't assign as much authority to them as the other books of the *Tanak*. This widely diverse third division of the Old Testament includes the poetic books of Psalms, Proverbs, and Job; the books referred to as the festival scrolls of Ruth, Song of Songs, Lamentations, and Esther; the apocalyptic Book of Daniel; and the priestly histories of Ezra, Nehemiah, and 1 and 2 Chronicles.

The Book of Psalms is a compilation of 150 wonderful poems that were collected over a period of centuries. These psalms are sometimes divided into seven different types: psalms of wisdom, meditation, and/or instruction; psalms of lament and petition; psalms of blessing and cursing; royal or messianic psalms; psalms of thanksgiving; and perhaps the most prominent, hymns of praise. Psalm 19, the source of the focal text for this lesson, is one of these hymns of praise.

Do you find comfort, peace, and hope when you read the Psalms? How can you more effectively use the Book of Psalms in your devotional time with God and perhaps find even greater comfort and hope?

Finding God in Creation

Psalm 19 has traditionally been divided into two sections. The first six verses praise the glory of God's creation, while verses 7-14 exalt the righteousness and wisdom of God's law. The second section is sometimes further divided, the final four verses of the psalm focusing on the psalmist himself.

The psalm comes together in a beautiful way and makes a profound point. The righteousness of God's laws is built right into God's creation.

The apostle Paul made this point in his letter to the church in Rome. He argued that everyone will come under God's judgment. Everyone is without excuse. "Gentiles don't have the Law. But when they instinctively do what the Law requires they are a Law in themselves, though they don't have the Law. They show the proof of the Law written on their hearts, and their consciences affirm it" (Romans 2:14-15).

Anyone who observes God's magnificent, orderly creation surely must realize there is a Creator and an order to the universe. "Heaven is declaring God's glory," the psalmist affirmed (Psalm 19:1). But this psalm is not the only one that calls attention to God's majestic creation.

Many people consider Psalm 8 to be the first psalm of praise. It, too, celebrates God as Creator. "When I look up at your skies, at what your fingers made—the moon and the stars that you set firmly in place—what are human beings that you think about them; what are human beings that you pay attention to them?" (8:3-4).

Psalm 104 is another song of praise that focuses on God's creative work. It begins, "Let my whole being bless the LORD! LORD my God, how fantastic you are! You are clothed in glory and grandeur! You wear light like a robe;

you open the skies like a curtain. You build your lofty house on the waters; you make the clouds your chariot going around on the wings of the wind" (verses 1-3).

From one day to the next, the psalmist declared, God's creation speaks of God's glory "throughout the world" (19:4). Speech and words are not necessary; "their voices can't be heard" (verse 3). God's creative work is so magnificent, so grand, so unsurpassed, only God can be praised for it. And God has promised to be with us always. This is especially good news when we are facing adversity, affliction, and grief and are full of anxiety.

Where do you see God in the physical world around you? Do you find comfort and hope in the beauty of God's creation and as signs of God's presence?

Worship God, Not Creation

A few years ago, my wife and I took a vacation visiting many of the national parks in our Western states. We spent one night near Carlsbad Caverns. This area has some of the darkest skies in the country. That night, we drove out into an isolated area where there were no lights anywhere around us. We were amazed by the brightness and beauty of that night sky. I had not seen such a brilliant Milky Way since I was a child living in a rural area of Mississippi.

The psalmist, of course, lived long before electric lights and other distractions that pollute and obscure the sky. People in those days were far more familiar with the moon and stars than most of us today. That night, looking at the gorgeous array of stars shining over the Guadalupe Mountains of southeastern New Mexico, I thought of Psalm 19:1: "Heaven is declaring God's glory: the sky is proclaiming his handiwork."

Of course, people in Old Testament times were even more impressed with the closest star. Many ancient cultures worshiped the sun, with archaeological evidence of this going back as early as the Neolithic age. The Egyptians famously worshiped Ra, their sun god. Early Mesopotamians worshiped Utu, who later became known as Shamash, as their sun god. Early Hinduism had Surya, their sun god. In Aztec religion, extensive human sacrifice was demanded by the sun gods Huitzilopochtli and Tezcatlipoca.

The Old Testament includes numerous admonitions against worshiping the sun and other objects of the creation rather than the Creator. For example, Deuteronomy 4:19 warns, "Don't look to the skies, to the sun or the moon or the stars, all the heavenly bodies, and be led astray, worshipping and serving them." Job defended his faithfulness by insisting, "If I've looked at the sun when it shone, the moon, splendid as it moved; and my mind has been secretly enticed, and threw a kiss with my hand, that also is a punishable offense, because I would then be disloyal to God above" (Job 31:26-28).

The psalmist was well aware of those warnings. The author of Psalm 19 didn't worship the sun; he worshiped the One who created the sun.

After acknowledging how beautifully God's creation points to its Creator, he said, "Honoring the LORD is correct, lasting forever. The LORD's judgments are true. All of these are righteous! . . . No doubt about it: your servant is enlightened by them; there is great reward in keeping them" (Psalm 19:9, 11). He closed with words many of us probably know by heart: "Let the words of my mouth and the meditations of my heart be pleasing to you, LORD, my rock and my redeemer" (verse 14).

The lessons in this unit encourage us to nurture and develop the spiritual practice of singing or meditating on hymns and songs of praise. In addition to the psalms mentioned in this lesson, you may want to explore some of the other psalms of praise and thanksgiving, such as 23, 24, 34, 46, 93, 96–100, 103, 114, 115, 118, 145, 114, 115, 118, 131, 136, 139, and 150.

Online searches can provide resources and helps in singing the psalms. You might enjoy singing some of them to already familiar tunes or to tunes you compose. If you weren't familiar with the hymn "Never Alone," you can search for it online and listen to it.

Dear God, we see your majesty, wonder, beauty, and power in all of creation. Help us feel your presence when we look carefully at the world around us, and help us proclaim your glory by the lives we live; in Jesus' name we pray. Amen.

The Spiritual Practice of Singing

In my decades-long service as a pastor, nothing has caused as much conflict in my churches as the music we sing in our worship services. Nothing else even comes close. Many people want to sing the old hymns they grew up singing. Others want a contemporary worship service with more current musical styles. There are even great differences of opinion about what is good or appropriate music within these genres.

We will all probably never agree on what comprises appropriate music for worship, but most of us do agree that music is an important part of our worship experience. God's people have always sung songs of praise and worship.

Exodus 15 tells us after escaping from slavery in Egypt and crossing the Reed Sea, the Israelites sang to the Lord. "Then the prophet Miriam, Aaron's sister, took a tambourine in her hand. All the women followed her playing tambourines and dancing. . . . Sing to the LORD, for an overflowing victory!" (Exodus 15:20-21).

The Old Testament includes numerous references to singing. For example, 1 Chronicles 6:31-32 reads, "David put the following in charge of the music in the LORD's house after the chest was placed there. They ministered with song before the dwelling of the meeting tent, until Solomon built the LORD's temple in Jerusalem."

Matthew's Gospel indicates Jesus and his disciples didn't forsake this tradition. Jesus ended the Last Supper this way: "Then, after singing songs of praise, they went to the Mount of Olives" (Matthew 26:30). We know the early church often joined together in music. For example,

Paul wrote to the Colossians, "The word of Christ must live in you richly. Teach and warn each other with all wisdom by singing psalms, hymns, and spiritual songs. Sing to God with gratitude in your hearts" (Colossians 3:16).

Developing the spiritual practice of singing songs of praise is not simply about audible singing, it is about praising God. Even those who insist they "can't carry a tune in a bucket" can meditate on hymns and songs of praise to God.

This week, select a favorite hymn or chorus. Spend time each day replaying it in your head. Sing aloud if you are comfortable. Think about it throughout the week, and allow it to guide your personal worship of God.

Focal Passage: Isaiah 6:1-13
Background Text: Same
Purpose Statement: To respond affirmatively to God's call on our lives

Isaiah 6:1-13

¹In the year of King Uzziah's death, I saw the Lord sitting on a high and exalted throne, the edges of his robe filling the temple. ²Winged creatures were stationed around him. Each had six wings: with two they veiled their faces, with two their feet, and with two they flew about. ³They shouted to each other, saying:

"Holy, holy, holy is the LORD of heavenly forces!

All the earth is filled with God's glory!"

⁴The doorframe shook at the sound of their shouting, and the house was filled with smoke.

⁵I said, "Mourn for me; I'm ruined! I'm a man with unclean lips, and I live among a people with unclean lips. Yet I've seen the king, the LORD of heavenly forces!"

⁶Then one of the winged creatures flew to me, holding a glowing coal that he had taken from the altar with tongs. ⁷He touched my mouth and said, "See, this has touched your lips. Your guilt has departed, and your sin is removed."

⁸Then I heard the Lord's voice saying, "Whom should I send, and who will go for us?"

I said, "I'm here; send me."

⁹God said, "Go and say to this people:

Listen intently, but don't understand;
  look carefully, but don't comprehend.

¹⁰Make the minds of this people dull.
  Make their ears deaf and their eyes blind,
  so they can't see with their eyes
  or hear with their ears,
  or understand with their minds,
  and turn, and be healed."

¹¹I said, "How long, Lord?"

And God said, "Until cities lie ruined with no one living in them, until there are houses without people and the land is left devastated." ¹²The LORD will send the people far away, and the land will be completely abandoned. ¹³Even if one-tenth remain there, they will be burned again, like a terebinth or an oak, which when it is cut down leaves a stump. Its stump is a holy seed.

Key Verse: "Then I heard the Lord's voice saying, 'Whom should I send, and who will go for us?' I said, 'I'm here; send me'" (Isaiah 6:8).

A preacher friend of mine is well-known for saying "Context is everything" as a way to stress the importance of context when studying Scripture. There are indeed many passages in the Bible we will never correctly interpret unless we understand their context.

In the preceding lesson, we sought to place Psalm 19 in its proper context. Doing this will also help us understand and fully appreciate this week's text from the Book of Isaiah. Like last week's lesson, this lesson gives us a front-row seat into an individual's personal experience in God's presence.

Isaiah is the first book of what we sometimes call the Latter Prophets in the Hebrew Bible. There were earlier prophets, but not until the eighth century did the prophets' disciples begin to collect and record their oracles. The Latter Prophets is a collection, mostly written in poetry, that claims to be the oracles of individual, particular prophets.

The significance of the ancient Israelite prophets was in direct proportion to the political and ethical conditions of the Jewish people. In fact, most of what is found in the Latter Prophets seems to have been recorded in response to three major crises: the Assyrian threat, the Babylonian threat, and Jewish struggles during the postexilic period.

The earliest recorded prophetic writings came during the tremendous threats posed by the Assyrians in the latter half of the eighth century BC. The prophets Amos and Hosea first warned the people and their leaders in the northern kingdom of Israel that their lack of faithfulness to God and their failure to practice social justice would lead to divine retribution. Their warnings came to pass when Assyria conquered Israel and took the people into captivity. Just a few years later, Isaiah (sometimes referred to as Isaiah of Jerusalem) and Micah delivered a similar warning to the people of Judah.

In 612 BC, the Assyrian empire fell to the Babylonians, who became the new threat to Judah and the holy city of Jerusalem. This led to another group of important prophets.

Among these were Jeremiah and Ezekiel. Many modern scholars also include a prophet often called Second Isaiah.

In 539 BC, the Persians, under the leadership of Cyrus the Great, conquered the Babylonians. Cyrus had a more lenient attitude toward conquered people and so allowed any Jews who wished to return to their homeland to do so. The third great crisis that seems to have led to a major prophetic response was the Jews' difficult period of readjustment after their return. This is the setting for Haggai, Zechariah, Joel, Malachi, Ezra, Nehemiah, and the prophet many scholars call Third Isaiah.

While the early Israelite prophets were sometimes called seers, we should understand Old Testament prophets were not primarily prognosticators of future events. Their primary task was to speak to the people on behalf of God. This is in contrast to the role of the priests, whose primary task was to speak to God on behalf of the people. While the prophets sometimes predicted what would happen in the future if the people disobeyed God, their challenge was to hear and understand God's will for the present, and to communicate that divine will to the people.

The man we read about in Isaiah 6 lived in turbulent times. God called him to stand up and be counted, to risk his life to make a difference, to warn his people about the coming catastrophe if they didn't turn back to God. He was called to condemn their greed and insensitive indifference to the poor.

Many would describe our age as an age of chaos and turbulent times. I certainly feel that way at present as we shelter at home in the midst of a worldwide pandemic. Whatever the situation around us, we all are called by God to make a difference. Will we respond like Isaiah of Jerusalem by saying, "I'm here; send me?" (Isaiah 6:8).

The Book of Isaiah

The Book of Isaiah is quoted in the New Testament more than any other book. Traditionally, it has been assumed the entire book was written by the eighth-century prophet Isaiah. However, most modern scholars now believe different sections were written over a period of several hundred years.

Most of the first 39 chapters of the book are usually attributed to the prophet who lived in Jerusalem during the latter half of the eighth century. The major themes of this section are justice and righteous obedience to God. At times, Jeremiah was a close advisor to the Judean kings and continually advised them to depend on God and not more powerful allies.

Many scholars believe Chapters 40–55 were written during the Babylonian exile by a prophet sometimes referred to as Second Isaiah. This section expresses the hope Cyrus the Great would eventually allow the Jews to return to their homeland. It also repeatedly declares the monotheistic view of God that had so recently become a central tenant of the Jewish faith. Yahweh is not only the God of Israel; Yahweh is the one and only true God, Creator and Sustainer of all that is.

Chapters 56–66 appear to contain oracles from throughout the prophetic period. This includes the work of a postexilic prophet referred to by some as Third Isaiah.

Biblical prophets like Isaiah clearly lived in different times and under vastly different circumstances than we do. Their experiences with God as recorded in Scripture are probably unlike anything we have experienced.

What do you think we can learn from the prophets? How does understanding the context in which they lived and prophesied better help you understand their message?

Isaiah of Jerusalem

The eighth-century prophet Isaiah was also a priest who was probably serving in the Temple when he heard his call from God to be a prophet. He was active during the reigns of Uzziah, Jotham, Ahaz, and Hezekiah and may have prophesied for as many as 64 years. As a prophet, he advised the Judean kings during three major crises: the Syro-Ephraimite War (around 735–734 BC), Hezekiah's struggles with Assyria and his temptation to seek alliance with Egypt (around 701 BC), and the Assyrian invasion (at the turn of the century).

Isaiah was vitally concerned about Judah's unfaithfulness to Yahweh and believed this would lead to harsh consequences if they did not repent. He was also deeply concerned about issues of social justice. He repeatedly insisted God was not interested in their empty rituals or their meaningless religious professions. They needed to walk their talk.

Both of these themes are found prominently in Isaiah 1, which serves as an overview of the entire book (Isaiah 1:10-20): "I'm fed up with entirely burned offerings of rams and the fat of well-fed beasts. I don't want the blood of bulls, lambs, and goats," God told the people through Isaiah (1:11). God was clearly fed up (verses 15-17, 19-20).

What do you think God might say about our religious rituals and practices? Can you think of any practices or injustices to which God might respond, "Put an end to such evil; learn to do good. Seek justice: help the oppressed"?

Sights, Sounds, and Sensations

Isaiah 6 describes Isaiah's encounter with God and the specific and difficult call to him. Isaiah clearly saw

God "sitting on a high and exalted throne, the edges of his robe filling the temple" (verse 1), which suggests God's presence was so great, Isaiah was standing in the doorway looking in.

Around God's throne were "winged creatures" who, because they were in God's presence, had to cover their eyes and their feet with some of their wings. They used their remaining wings to fly around, all the while shouting affirmations of God's holiness and greatness.

Coming into God's presence, in fact, means encountering and experiencing God's holiness. What could be more awe-inspiring? "All the earth is filled with God's glory!" the winged creatures shouted (verse 3). God is so radically other, and the whole earth is full of God's powerful presence. The shouting of the winged creatures was such that the doorframes shook and "the house was filled with smoke" (verse 4), adding another layer of drama and intensity to Isaiah's divine encounter.

All of the sights and sounds and sensations pointing to God's holiness served also to point by contrast to the sin and guilt of the people. As a priest entering the Temple, Isaiah would've been ceremonially clean, but he mourned his own "unclean lips" (verse 5). God's holiness and majesty were so great, Isaiah saw himself as being in the same condition as the people he represented.

The seraph's ritual of purification assured Isaiah his guilt [had] departed, and [his] sin [had been] removed" (verses 6-7). That put Isaiah in the position of hearing and responding to what would happen next.

When have you been keenly aware of God's unique holiness? What were the circumstances? How did you respond?

God Speaks

Although Scripture does not suggest God spoke directly to Isaiah at this point, God did, in fact, speak: "Whom should I send, and who will go for us?" (Isaiah 6:8). Without knowing any details, Isaiah responded, "I'm here; send me." It was only after saying this that Isaiah received any details about his assignment.

It sounds strange to our ears. God told Isaiah to tell the people to "listen intently," but not understand; look but not comprehend. And "make the minds of this people dull. Make their ears deaf and their eyes blind, so they can't see with their eyes or hear with their ears, or understand with their minds, and turn, and be healed" (verse 10).

What, exactly, was God asking Isaiah to do? Essentially, Isaiah was to prevent the people from repenting. Repentance at this point was not possible. Without the context of all of Isaiah 1–39, this sounds incredibly harsh. But the people had been repeatedly warned. They had had plenty of opportunities to turn back to God, and they had refused. Now they must face the consequences of their choices.

"How long?" Isaiah asked God. The answer was shocking. Not until cities had been "ruined" and were deserted, the land was "devastated," and the people were sent to live "far away," God said. Isaiah's encounter with God in the Temple was so moving and powerful, he said yes to God's call before he had any idea what it would involve.

Do you think Isaiah would have so readily responded to God's call if he had known the message God wanted him to deliver? Have you ever responded to God with an open-ended yes without knowing any details? What were the results of that response?

Our Response

The same God who called Isaiah calls each of us to follow Jesus Christ, to become his disciples, to live by his teachings and example, and to lead others into that relationship. Each of us has a place in God's divine plan, a role to fill in growing God's kingdom on earth.

Paul wrote, "He gave some apostles, some prophets, some evangelists, and some pastors and teachers. His purpose was to equip God's people for the work of serving and building up the body of Christ until we all reach the unity of faith and knowledge of God's Son. God's goal is for us to become mature adults—to be fully grown, measured by the standard of the fullness of Christ" (Ephesians 4:11-13).

The spiritual practice we are encouraged to engage during this unit is singing (or meditating on) a hymn of praise. We have already seen the psalms repeatedly encourage us to use music to praise God. However, there are also many other passages of Scripture that encourage this spiritual practice. Consider: Chronicles 5:13; Amos 6:5; Ephesians 5:19; Colossians 3:16; Hebrews 2:12; Revelation 14:3-4. You might also want to continue to read or sing some of your favorite psalms.

What specific things has God called you to do in building up the body of Christ?

Dear God, we live in chaotic times. Forgive us when we fail to hear and respond to your call on our lives and when we fail to live by your laws. Show us how to live faithfully each day; in Jesus' name we pray. Amen.

Focal Passage: Mark 9:2-8
Background Text: Mark 9:2-13
Purpose Statement: To understand how listening to God can radically change our lives

Mark 9:2-13

²Six days later Jesus took Peter, James, and John, and brought them to the top of a very high mountain where they were alone. He was transformed in front of them, ³and his clothes were amazingly bright, brighter than if they had been bleached white. ⁴Elijah and Moses appeared and were talking with Jesus. ⁵Peter reacted to all of this by saying to Jesus, "Rabbi, it's good that we're here. Let's make three shrines—one for you, one for Moses, and one for Elijah." ⁶He said this because he didn't know how to respond, for the three of them were terrified.

⁷Then a cloud overshadowed them, and a voice spoke from the cloud, "This is my Son, whom I dearly love. Listen to him!" ⁸Suddenly, looking around, they no longer saw anyone with them except Jesus.

Key Verse: "Then a cloud overshadowed them, and a voice spoke from the cloud, 'This is my son, Whom I dearly love. Listen to him!'" (Mark 9:7).

A parishioner once talked to me about an adult son who had had a lifetime of struggles with psychological issues. He expressed frustration that his son would seek his advice but then ignore it if it didn't align with what he wanted to hear. The son would get angry, curse him, and often even refuse to speak to him for months. It seemed to me in those situations, the young man was not seeking the father's advice but the father's affirmation and approval.

Sometimes we treat God the same way. We claim to be listening, but we just want divine approval and the benefits God provides. We want the inheritance, but we don't want God to tell us how to live. We would rather do it our way.

My former parishioner's son continues to struggle with failed marriages, and he has little to no relationship with his child. He has trouble keeping a job, and at times he has had to live out of the car his father helped him purchase. But he still insists he knows best, largely ignoring God and those in his life who could help him make better decisions. Imagine how different his life might have been had he formed the habit of listening to his father and to God.

We ignore God at our own peril. Our Scripture text for this lesson, the account of Jesus' transfiguration, is an important reminder of Jesus' unique relationship with God and an explicit directive to listen to Jesus' teachings and God's voice.

A Pattern of Prayer

Numerous Gospel accounts report Jesus going off by himself and spending time in prayer, listening to the divine voice. Luke's Gospel tells us Jesus spent a great deal of time alone with God seeking guidance in the midst of the heavy demands made on his life: "News of him spread even more and huge crowds gathered to listen and to be healed from their illnesses. But Jesus would withdraw to deserted places for prayer" (Luke 5:15-16). Before Jesus chose his inner circle of disciples, he spent all night seeking God's direction (Luke 6:12-13).

In Luke's account of Jesus' Transfiguration, he tells us it was for the very reason of prayer that he went up on the mountain where he was transformed: "About eight days after Jesus said these things, he took Peter, John, and James, and went up on a mountain to pray. As he was praying, the appearance of his face changed and his clothes flashed white like lightning" (Luke 9:28-29).

But we don't need to leave Mark's Gospel to see how important prayer was to Jesus. In the first chapter, Mark tells us, "Early in the morning, well before sunrise, Jesus rose and went to a deserted place where he could be alone in prayer" (Mark 1:35). Jesus seems to have done this, at least partially, in response to the increasing demands being made upon him.

"Simon and those with him tracked him down. When they found him, they told him, 'Everyone's looking for you!' " The busier Jesus became, the more important it was for him to spend time alone with God, seeking strength and direction.

After a busy time of healing, "Jesus went out beside the lake again," likely needing some time alone with God. But the crowds followed him there. On another occasion, after dismissing the crowds and sending his disciples ahead of him toward Bethsaida, "Jesus went up onto a mountain to pray" (6:46). Just hours before facing the cross, "Jesus and his disciples came to a place called Gethsemane. Jesus said to them, 'Sit here while I pray" (14:32).

Jesus could do God's will only if he knew it, and he could only know God's will if he spent quiet time listening. The same is true for us. In order to live the way God wants us to live and do with our lives what God wants us to do, we must spend time in prayer, listen for God's voice, and seek to discern and understand God's directions.

God not only spoke to Jesus. Scripture reveals God speaks to us. God not only spoke to Jesus on the mountain that day of the Transfiguration; God also spoke to Peter, James, and John who were with him that day. Jesus invited them to go with him to the mountaintop because he was training them, mentoring them, and teaching them by his example. One important lesson they needed to learn was to listen for the voice of God.

Do you have specific times set aside for prayer? When do you pray? How much of your prayer time involves you talking to God? How much involves you listening for the voice of God?

Why These Three?

It's important to note, according to Mark, Jesus' transfiguration took place "six days later" (Mark 9:2), following a time Jesus and his disciples had spent in "the villages near Caesarea Phlippi" (8:27).

On that occasion, Jesus asked his disciples about his identity: "Who do people say that I am?" (8:27). After they reported what others had said, he asked, "And what about you? Who do you say that I am?" Notice that Peter answered perceptively and correctly, saying, "You are the Christ" (8:29).

It was Peter, along with James and John, Jesus took with him "to the top of a very high mountain where they were alone" (9:2). These were the same three disciples who were with Jesus when he healed Jairus's daughter (5:37).

Why these three? Were they exceptionally insightful or faithful? Not always. Peter had, just prior to this experience, been scolded for rejecting the idea Jesus had to suffer (8:33). Only a short time later, James and John would request that Jesus allow them to sit on either side of him when he entered his glory (10:35-37), showing that their concern was not for service but for greatness.

Only a few chapters later in Mark's Gospel, we read that all three of these disciples could not stay awake and pray with Jesus during his agony in the garden of Gethsemane (14:33-41). We may wonder then, if the divine instruction they received on the mountaintop that day with Jesus came back later to trouble them (9:7).

Why do you think Jesus took only Peter, James, and John with him to the top of the mountain and none of the other disciples?

Awe-Inspiring Transformation

More so than either of the other two Synoptic Gospels, Mark's Gospel moves quickly, even urgently, toward the cross and Jesus' resurrection. Bible scholars have noted it uses the word "immediately" some 40 times. We notice this straightforward, hurried approach in Mark's report of

Jesus' Transfiguration. In just two short verses, Mark succinctly described what happened after the trio of disciples and Jesus got to the top of the mountain: "He was transformed in front of them, and his clothes were amazingly bright, brighter than if they had been bleached white" (Mark 9:2-3).

The KJV, the NIV, the NRSV, and the NASB all use the word "transfigured" to describe what happened to Jesus, while the CEB uses the word "transformed." Both are accurate and indicate that Jesus' external appearance dramatically changed, causing him to become stunningly bright.

But that was not all. Mark had been careful to note that Jesus, Peter, James, and John were alone on the mountaintop (verse 2). But, suddenly, Moses and Elijah "appeared and were talking with Jesus" (verse 4).

Scripture doesn't tell us what they were talking about. Jewish tradition expected that one or both of these figures would return to earth when God's kingdom arrived. And as most scholars have pointed out, Moses represented the Law, while Elijah represented the Prophets. While Moses and Elijah were the only people in the Old Testament who saw God's full glory, they were both prevented from seeing God's face. Here, they saw God's face as Jesus, right in front of them.

True to his often impetuous nature, Peter immediately came up with a plan. "Rabbi," he said to Jesus, "it's good that we're here. Let's make three shrines—one for you, one for Moses, and one for Elijah." And Mark just as immediately tells us that Peter "said this because he didn't know how to respond, for the three of them were terrified" (verses 5-6).

Throughout Scripture, theophanies—visible manifestations of God—usually happen on mountains. Have you ever had a close experience with God while on a mountain? What happened, and how did it change you and your relationship with God?

Divine Instruction

As if the disciples were not terrified enough, what happened next most certainly created more fear in them. A "cloud overshadowed them, and a voice spoke from the cloud, 'This is my Son, whom I dearly love. Listen to him!'" (Mark 9:7).

Clouds in Scripture often symbolize God's presence, and should there have been any question in the disciples' minds about what was happening, God spoke to them from the cloud with an affirmation of Jesus' identity and a specific instruction: Listen. Listen to Jesus. Implicit in the meaning of the word used for "listen" is "to comprehend, to understand." And then, seemingly just as quickly as these awe-inspiring events had happened, the three disciples discovered as they looked around that they were again alone with Jesus (verse 8).

Jesus had been deliberately and carefully preparing his disciples for the fact that he would face suffering on the cross and reassuring them of his identity as the Messiah, God's Son, the Savior. How would this experience affect these disciples in the coming days and weeks? How did it change their understanding of Jesus and their relationship to God through him? The divine instruction was simple yet profound: Listen.

Sometimes when I teach or preach about listening to God, someone will complain that they try to listen, but they don't feel that God ever says anything to them, or perhaps they can't hear God. In response, I usually ask them a question: "Have you done the last thing God asked you to do?"

Often the individual never answers that question. They may ignore it, or they may say they have never heard God ask them to do anything. A few will honestly admit they probably haven't. I then ask another question: "Why would God speak to you if you consistently ignore what God has to say?"

Like many Christians, years ago, I began using a journal that included, among other things, an extensive prayer list. Each day during my prayer time, I would go over this list in detail with God. After several weeks of doing this, I began to feel God was well aware of everything on my list. I had a strong feeling God was saying to me, "I know about you and your list. How about just sitting still for a moment and listen to me."

Over time, I learned if I sat still and quiet for a while I could hear God's voice as I had never before. Through this, I've learned I don't have to be talking all the time, and I am not frustrated if I don't always hear anything in particular from God. Sometimes I simply sit with an awareness of the divine presence and listen carefully in case God does have something specific to tell me.

Certainly, in our relationship with God, we have many things we think we need to tell God, and God stands ready to hear us. But as the disciples learned on the mountaintop with Jesus that day, we also need to listen to God, to develop a sensitivity to God's voice, and to respond to what God says to us. We need to listen.

Which do you find it easier to do: talk to God or listen for God's voice? What are specific things you can do to better hear when God speaks to you?

Dear God, help us open our hearts and minds to sense your presence, to feel your love, and to hear your voice. Help us comprehend the mission you give us and renew our commitment to your call; in Jesus' name we pray. Amen.

Focal Passage: Exodus 34:29-35
Background Text: Same
Purpose Statement: To strengthen our resolve to make listening to God a priority

Exodus 34:29-35

²⁹Moses came down from Mount Sinai. As he came down from the mountain with the two covenant tablets in his hand, Moses didn't realize that the skin of his face shone brightly because he had been talking with God. ³⁰When Aaron and all the Israelites saw the skin of Moses' face shining brightly, they were afraid to come near him. ³¹But Moses called them closer. So Aaron and all the leaders of the community came back to him, and Moses spoke with them. ³²After that, all the Israelites came near as well, and Moses commanded them everything that the LORD had spoken with him on Mount Sinai. ³³When Moses finished speaking with them, he put a veil over his face. ³⁴Whenever Moses went into the LORD's presence to speak with him, Moses would take the veil off until he came out again. When Moses came out and told the Israelites what he had been commanded, ³⁵the Israelites would see that the skin of Moses' face was shining brightly. So Moses would put the veil on his face again until the next time he went in to speak with the LORD.

Key Verse: "After that, all the Israelites came near as well, and Moses commanded them everything that the LORD had spoken with him on Mount Sinai" (Exodus 34:32).

If you have attended church most or all of your life, you have probably picked up on some of the vocabulary. We use words and phrases such as *faith*, *grace*, *mercy*, *salvation*, and *eternal life*; and we have pretty good ideas about what we mean when we use them. The word *glory* is like that. We hear it regularly in church. "Holy, holy, holy Lord, God of power and might, heaven and earth are full of your glory," we say as part of our Communion liturgy. "All honor and glory is yours, almighty Father."[1]

"For the kingdom, the power, and the glory are yours now and for ever," we pray in the Lord's Prayer.

The word *glory* is woven throughout our hymns and worship songs. "Glory Be to the Father," and "Glory to God in the Highest," we sing. "To God Be the Glory," we affirm. "Give him the glory, great things he hath done."[2]

But what is glory? What do we mean when we talk about God's glory? How would you explain it to someone who was new to our insider vocabulary?

Fellow ADULT BIBLE STUDIES writer Randy Cross explains it this way: "Glory describes the presence, the radiance, the total environment surrounding God. Glory is the unbridled holiness and sacredness of God, something we can only wish to reflect, but are unable to claim ourselves. True glory is a singular expression only of God's being."

Biblical writers described or referred to the glory of God in a number of ways. "To the Israelites, the LORD's glorious presence looked like a blazing fire on top of the mountain," we read in Exodus 24:17. "Heaven is declaring God's glory," the psalmist wrote. "The sky is proclaiming his handiwork" (Psalm 19:1). "The Word became flesh and made his home among us," declared John in his Gospel. "We have seen his glory, glory like that of a father's only son, full of grace and truth" (John 1:14).

Glory, we must conclude, is powerful, and it points to and reveals God! Often, in the biblical narrative it is associated with light and brightness. It signifies the holiness and mystery of God entering into human experience. And glory has an amazing effect on those who come in contact with it.

That was the case for Moses, and in turn, for the people of Israel. Beholding God's glory, being in the presence of God in all God's holiness, changed everything for them. And it changes everything for us.

A Little Context

While our Focal Passage comes from Exodus 34 and begins when "Moses came down from Mount Sinai" (Exodus 34:29), it's important we understand why he had made this particular trek. You probably remember the story. Moses had previously gone up the mountain, where God gave him a number of instructions. "When God finished speaking with Moses on Mount Sinai, God gave him the two covenant tablets, the stone tablets written by God's finger" (31:18).

But Moses stayed on the mountain longer than the Israelites were willing to wait. "The people saw that Moses was taking a long time to come down from the mountain. They gathered around Aaron and said to him, 'Come on! Make us gods who can lead us. As for this man Moses who brought us up out of the land of Egypt, we don't have a clue what has happened to him'" (32:1).

And you probably know what happened next. To appease the people, Aaron fashioned a bull calf out of their gold jewelry, which the people worshiped. God, of course, was furious: "Let my fury burn and devour them," God said to Moses (32:10). After Moses pleaded with God to spare the people, "the LORD changed his mind about the terrible things he said he would do to his people" (32:14).

Moses went down the mountain, carrying the tablets on which God had written the divine instructions. But when he saw the people worshiping the gold bull calf, he was outraged. He threw down the tablets, breaking them into pieces.

Exodus 32:35 declares, "Then the LORD sent a plague on the people because of what they did with the bull calf that Aaron made." Exodus 33 opens by saying, "The LORD said to Moses, 'Go and leave this place, you and the people whom you brought up out of the land of Egypt. Go to the land I promised to Abraham, Isaac, and Jacob. . . . But I won't go up with you because I would end up destroying you along the way since you are a stubborn people'" (33:1-3).

Recall much earlier in Exodus when Moses had the encounter with God at the burning bush. There, God called the future lawgiver to go back to Egypt and take the Israelites out of bondage. Moses responded, "Who am I to go to Pharaoh and to bring the Israelites out of Egypt?" (3:11). God then promised, "I'll be with you. And this will show you that I'm the one who sent you. After you bring the people out of Egypt, you will come back here and worship God on this mountain" (3:12).

Moses must surely have remembered this promise when God said, as reported in Chapter 33, "But I won't go up with you." It was vital to Moses to know God was with him and would guide him in all he did. The following verses in Chapter 33 tell how Moses set up a tent where he continued to meet with God to receive instructions. There, he pleaded with God to "show me your ways so that I may know you and so that you may really approve of me" (33:13). God finally said, "'I'll go myself, and I'll help you'" (33:14). What a relief that must've been for Moses!

Do you have a place where you regularly meet with God, seeking his instructions and help?

Another Mountain Trek

Exodus 34 opens by telling us, "The LORD said to Moses, 'Cut two stone tablets like the first ones. I'll write on these tablets the words that were on the first tablets, which you broke into pieces'" (Exodus 34:1).

God further instructed Moses to return to the top of the mountain, and "the LORD came down in the cloud and stood there with him" (verse 5), proclaiming more of God's character to Moses, offering forgiveness, and renewing the broken covenant. "Moses was there with the LORD forty days and forty nights. He didn't eat any bread or drink any water. He wrote on the tablets the words of the covenant, the ten words" (verse 28).

It was when Moses came down from the mountain that something amazing, something awe-inspiring happened! "The skin of his face shone brightly because he had been talking with God. When Aaron and all the Israelites saw the skin of Moses' face shining brightly, they were afraid to come near him" (verses 29-30).

It was just too much! The people responded in fear, having never seen anything like this before. They were accustomed to God speaking to Moses and Moses reporting to them what God had said, giving them the divine commands and instructions. Those exchanges involved God speaking, Moses listening, then Moses speaking and the people listening. But never had they had a visual effect such as this!

Something had happened to Moses, something now reflected from his face. Moses saw God's glory and in turn, the people of Israel saw it, too.

When have you seen something that affirmed God's presence with you? What did you see, and how did it affect your understanding of God?

The Veil

In spite of their initial fear, Moses convinced "Aaron and all the leaders of the community" to come closer to him so that he could tell them "everything that the LORD had spoken with him on Mount Sinai" (Exodus 34:31-32). Then "he put a veil over his face" (verse 33). Bible commentators are uncertain as to the veil's purpose. Was it to protect the Israelites? Or was it to shield God's glow from common things that would seem to lessen its significance? Perhaps it was both.

While we're uncertain as to its significance, it's clear the veil was part of the communication process between God and Moses, and Moses and the people. Each time Moses spoke with God or with the people, he removed the veil, then put it back on until another time of communication (verses 33-35). The absence of the veil clearly conveyed in visual form the presence, power, and authority of God, in whom Israel found her identity. Without God, Israel would not be Israel.

One of the lessons the people of Israel had to learn, and one we must also learn, is while God is gracious, compassionate, and loving, God also makes arduous demands and requires total allegiance. An important part of their ongoing relationship with God was confession, repentance, and forgiveness.

When Moses discovered the people had worshiped a golden image, he said to them, "You've committed a terrible sin. So now I will go up to the LORD. Maybe I can arrange reconciliation on account of your sin" (32:30). When Moses returned, as we have already seen, he informed the people that God was so upset with them, he had refused to go any further with them. We are then told, "When the people heard the bad news, they were sorry" (33:4).

One of the things that became clear to the people, and becomes clear to us, is that when we are in God's presence, we become acutely aware of our sins, our shortcomings, our disobedience. The brightness of God's glory invades the darkest corners of our lives and exposes those things we may try to hide. Whatever those things might be, God stands ready to forgive us and restore our relationship so we can listen to and walk into the future God has prepared for us.

In what areas of your life does the brightness of God's glory need to shine? Is there something you need to confess to God and for which you need to seek forgiveness?

Entering God's Presence With Singing

The spiritual practice our lessons encourage during this unit is singing or meditating on hymns of praise. Many people find that singing or listening to music helps them enter into God's presence.

It's easy, unfortunately, for us to drift away from a close relationship in which we acutely feel God's presence. Instead of treating our faith as business as usual, our relationship with God requires intentionality. Each day offers us a new opportunity to enter the light of God's glory and presence, give ourselves fully to God, listen to what God is calling us to do, and ask God to use us to reflect the divine glory to those around us.

The Psalms, the worship book of the people of Israel, offers us songs and hymns of praise that can take us more fully into God's presence. Select a different psalm of praise each day this week to read, pray, or sing. Enter into God's presence through the Psalms, and ask God to reflect the divine presence to those around you so they will know you have been in God's presence.

Dear God, we thank you that you do not hide yourself from us and that you know us and want us to know you. Expose the areas of our lives that need your forgiveness. Help us to listen to you more closely and walk with you more faithfully; in Jesus' name we pray. Amen.

Focal Passage: Revelation 19:1-10
Background Text: Same
Purpose Statement: To acknowledge that only God is worthy of our worship

Revelation 19:1-10

¹After this I heard what sounded like a huge crowd in heaven. They said,

"Hallelujah! The salvation and glory and power of our God!

²His judgments are true and just,

   because he judged the great prostitute,

     who ruined the earth by her whoring,

     and he exacted the penalty for the blood of his servants

     from her hand."

³Then they said a second time,

"Hallelujah! Smoke goes up from her forever and always."

⁴The twenty-four elders and the four living creatures fell down and worshipped God, who is seated on the throne, and they said, "Amen. Hallelujah!"

⁵Then a voice went out from the throne and said,

"Praise our God, all you his servants,

   and you who fear him, both small and great."

⁶And I heard something that sounded like a huge crowd, like rushing water and powerful thunder. They said,

"Hallelujah! The Lord our God, the Almighty,

   exercised his royal power!

[7]Let us rejoice and celebrate, and give him the glory,
for the wedding day of the Lamb has come,
and his bride has made herself ready.
[8]She was given fine, pure white linen to wear,
for the fine linen is the saints' acts of justice."

[9]Then the angel said to me, "Write this: Favored are those who have been invited to the wedding banquet of the Lamb." He said to me, "These are the true words of God." [10]Then I fell at his feet to worship him. But he said, "Don't do that! I'm a servant just like you and your brothers and sisters who hold firmly to the witness of Jesus. Worship God! The witness of Jesus is the spirit of prophecy!"

Key Verse: "Then I fell at his feet to worship him. But he said, 'Don't do that! I'm a servant just like you and your brothers and sisters who hold firmly to the witness of Jesus. Worship God! The witness of Jesus is the spirit of prophecy!' " (Revelation 19:10).

If you are a member of a choir or an ensemble that helps lead worship music, you know the important role music plays in worship. Even those who claim they "can't carry a tune in a bucket" can appreciate the beautiful sounds that help focus our minds and hearts on God, the object of our worship. Imagine what worship would be like if music were not a part. Certainly, the spoken word and silence are important in worship, but music brings something to worship such that we notice when it is absent.

For many people, nothing is more moving than the familiar "Hallelujah Chorus" from Handel's "Messiah." Throughout the chorus, the word *hallelujah* resounds, calling us to joyful praise of God. As some who have sung the chorus with massive choirs affirm, you can't sing it loudly enough!

Leading up to the chorus, members of the audience fill with anticipation as the full-bodied choir sings its way through the story of the prophets foretelling the Messiah's coming, the annunciation to the shepherds of Christ's birth, Christ's passion and death, his resurrection and ascension, and the spreading of the gospel throughout the world. Then the chorus brings everyone to their feet, a triumphant declaration of God's power, glory, and authority.

Perhaps other songs have a similar effect on you, such as "Praise God, from whom all blessings flow; praise God all creatures here below: Alleluia! Alleluia! Praise God, the source of all our gifts! Praise Jesus Christ, whose power uplifts! Praise the Spirit, Holy Spirit! Alleluia! Alleluia! Alleluia!"[1] Can't you hear the melody, even as you read the words?

Music in our worship reminds us God alone is worthy of our worship. Calls to worship run throughout both Testaments of Scripture, from the Psalms and the prophets of old to the apostle Paul, to the author of Revelation. This lesson is the last of five that look at awe-inspiring biblical events that call for the praise and worship of God.

We first considered by exploring Psalm 19 how taking in the beauty of creation brings us closer to and calls us to worship God. Then we saw Isaiah awed by God's presence in the Temple, humble worship the only appropriate response.

The following lesson led us up the mountain with Jesus, where we experienced through Peter, James, and

John the mystery and majesty of Jesus' transfiguration. Lesson 8 reminded us God's radiance and glory can be mediated to us through other people, and how we can, in turn, reflect God's presence to others. In this lesson, we will "join the choir of angels" as we offer praise and worship to God.

Reason to Rejoice?

Most people agree that understanding the Book of Revelation is challenging, but don't let that stop you from reading it. The fact is Revelation offers us important lessons about how to live faithfully in a world that, in many ways, is just as troubled as the world in which John, identified as the author, wrote.

Such faithful, even joyful, living is possible when we recognize that our God is more powerful than the circumstances in which we find ourselves, even the most difficult and troubling ones. Those circumstances do not have to define us, and they will not have the last word. God will.

Most scholars believe Revelation's author to have been a John other than the apostle John. He received and was instructed to write down a series of visions during the time of the Roman emperor Domitian, who reigned from AD 81-96. Domitian severely persecuted Christians, charging them with all kinds of crimes, including failure to support the worship of the Roman emperor. Finding hope was difficult for them, and rejoicing was even harder.

John's visions raised questions these Christians certainly had concerning God's justice, when God would punish the wicked, and how God would prove the innocence of those who are righteous. John's visions reveal

God indeed punishing those who aligned themselves with the dragon (Satan) and showing that those who are righteous are victorious.

At the same time, the visions reveal ongoing heavenly worship that praises God's unrivaled authority and justice. This lesson focuses on a few verses toward the end of the book that show us "a huge crowd in heaven" (Revelation 19:1) raising their voices in praise to God.

When have you struggled to find hope? What circumstances have you faced that have made it difficult for you to offer praise and worship to God?

Praise God!

John's vision recorded in Revelation 19:1-10 seems to be in response to the call of the angel in Revelation 18:20. There, the angel tells God's "saints, apostles, and prophets" to "rejoice" over the destruction of Rome. At its core, this is a call to recognize God's supreme authority. Not even the mighty, wealthy, arrogant Roman Empire was a match for the almighty God.

"Hallelujah!" the heavenly chorus sings, praising God for "true and just" judgments. *Hallelujah* is a Hebrew phrase that means "Praise God." The reference to "the great prostitute" in Revelation 19:2 is to Rome. You may recall Old Testament writers used the imagery of prostitution to warn and judge those who were led astray by idols and great wealth.

Then the huge crowd "said a second time, Hallelujah!" (Revelation 19:3), and John reports he saw "the twenty-four elders and the four living creatures" fall down in worship to God, saying, "Amen. Hallelujah" (verse 4).

Another call then came from a voice on the throne to "praise our God, all you his servants, and you who fear him, both small and great" (verse 5). This was followed by "something that sounded like a huge crowd, like rushing water and powerful thunder" (verse 6) that praised God and God's sovereignty. They called for rejoicing and celebration and announced the "wedding day of the Lamb has come, and his bride has made herself ready" (verse 7).

Prophets—including Isaiah, Ezekiel, and Hosea—employed the image of Israel as God's bride (Isaiah 54:6; Ezekiel 16:7-8; Hosea 2:16). New Testament writers refined that image so Christ is the bridegroom and the church is the bride (Mark 2:19-20; 2 Corinthians 11:2; Ephesians 5:25). Here in John's vision, God gives the bride a "pure white" wedding gown made of linen, symbolizing "the saints' acts of justice" (Revelation 19:8).

When have you been filled with the urge to offer praise to God? Was it when something delightful or good happened? Maybe it was at the birth of a child. Or perhaps someone you love was mercifully and miraculously healed from a life-threatening health condition. It could've been as a result of something in nature, like a beautiful sunrise or a sunset.

But perhaps your urge to worship God came as a result of a terrible experience, maybe a personal failure when you realized God's mercy, love, and forgiveness. It could have come following a devastating personal loss, when you unmistakably felt God's presence with you.

Certainly, life hands us experiences of both kinds—good and bad. And in everything, we have the assurance of

God's love, presence, power, and sovereignty. In the end, God is triumphant and deserves our worship and praise. That realization causes us to join the heavenly chorus and sing, "Hallelujah!"

When has someone or something outside of you compelled you to worship God? What were the circumstances? How did you respond?

Worship God!

This vision of John ended with instructions from the angel to write, "Favored are those who have been invited to the wedding banquet of the Lamb" (Revelation 19:9). So moved was John, he "fell at [the angel's] feet to worship him" (verse 10).

"Don't do that!" the angel admonished him. "Worship God!" (verse 10).

Perhaps John thought the angel was some kind of divine figure, since earlier he had heard a voice from the throne. We can't be sure. But the angel refused to accept John's attempts at worshiping him. "I'm a servant just like you and your brothers and sisters who hold firmly to the witness of Jesus," the angel told him.

The angel's words to John to worship God are words for us, too. God alone is worthy of our worship. God alone deserves our praise.

The spiritual practice we have been developing during these lessons involves singing or meditating on hymns of praise. This week, allow these words to lead you as you worship God.

"Praise to the Lord, the Almighty, the King of creation!
O my soul, praise him, for he is thy health and salvation!
All ye who hear, now to his temple draw near;
Join me in glad adoration! . . .
"Praise to the Lord! O let all that is in me adore him!
All that hath life and breath, come now with praises before him!
Let the amen sound from his people again;
Gladly forever adore him."[2]

Dear God, help us recognize your power and authority and sense your presence and protection, even and especially when circumstances around us cause us to doubt. Remind us you alone are worthy of our worship; in Jesus' name. Amen.

[1]*Hymnal*, 94.
[2]*Hymnal*, 139

Daily Bible Readings (Unit 3)

January 31
Philippians
4:10-13

February 1
John 13:3-8

February 2
John 13:12-17

February 3
John 15:4-5

February 4
Psalm 90:14-17

February 5
Proverbs 16:1-3

February 6
Deuteronomy
6:4-9; Matthew
22:34-40

February 7
Deuteronomy
10:17-22

February 8
1 Peter 2:11-12

February 9
John 15:9-11

February 10
1 John 2:9-11

February 11
Daniel 12:1-4

February 12
Isaiah 42:5-7

February 13
Matthew 5:14-16

February 14
Matthew 7:21-23

February 15
Matthew 6:5-6

February 16
Isaiah 29:13-14

February 17
Luke 6:46-49

February 18
Ezekiel 13:8-11

February 19
1 John 2:3-6

February 20
James 1:19-27

February 21
Genesis 12:1-3

February 22
2 Corinthians
5:11-15

February 23
2 Corinthians
5:16-21

February 24
Isaiah 2:2-3

February 25
Zechariah 8:20-23

February 26
Revelation
11:15-16

February 27
Matthew 28:16-20

Unit 3
Show and Tell

In this final unit of lessons, we will explore ways we can participate in God's work in our world. We will be reminded God doesn't save us to "sit and soak," but for mission and ministry, to make a difference in our world. We aren't saved by works, but that doesn't mean God doesn't assign us plenty of work to do. The author of John's Gospel quotes Jesus: "I assure you that whoever believes in me will do the works that I do. They will do even greater works than these because I am going to the Father" (John 14:12).

In Lesson 10, we will revisit the Great Commandments, discover what it means to love God, and better understand how Scripture encourages us to express that love. We will recall the importance of the *Shema* in Jewish tradition and how Christians have sought to obey the Great Commandments.

In Lesson 11, we will explore how our actions make God's glory and love for the world evident. We will reflect on what it means to be the light of the world. It is a sobering thought that others in our world often judge God by our actions. Do we express our love in a way others see God's love in us?

Lesson 12 takes us to the Book of James and reminds us we "must be doers of the word and not only hearers." It is not enough to talk the talk, James says. We have to walk the walk if we are to be genuine disciples of Jesus.

In our final lesson this quarter, we will be reminded it is not only our job as followers of Jesus to be disciples, but it is also our job to make disciples. Our text is a passage from the Gospel of Matthew we know as the Great Commission because this is the great mission God has given every Christian.

Focal Passages: Deuteronomy 6:4-9; Matthew 22:34-40
Background Text: Same
Purpose Statement: To renew our commitment to the Great Commandments

Deuteronomy 6:4-9

⁴Israel, listen! Our God is the LORD! Only the LORD! ⁵Love the LORD your God with all your heart, all your being, and all your strength. ⁶These words that I am commanding you today must always be on your minds. ⁷Recite them to your children. Talk about them when you are sitting around your house and when you are out and about, when you are lying down and when you are getting up. ⁸Tie them on your hand as a sign. They should be on your forehead as a symbol. ⁹Write them on your house's doorframes and on your city's gates.

Matthew 22:34-40

³⁴When the Pharisees heard that Jesus had left the Sadducees speechless, they met together. ³⁵One of them, a legal expert, tested him. ³⁶"Teacher, what is the greatest commandment in the Law?"

³⁷He replied, "You must love the Lord your God with all your heart, with all your being, and with all your mind. ³⁸This is the first and greatest commandment. ³⁹And the second is like it: You must love your neighbor as you love yourself. ⁴⁰All the Law and the Prophets depend on these two commands."

Key Verse: "He replied, You must love the Lord your God with all your heart, with all your being, and with all your mind. This is the first and greatest commandment" (Matthew 22:37-38).

Many churches around the world are in decline, and The United Methodist Church is certainly no exception. At the founding of our nation in the late eighteenth century, Methodists were few in number. However, the early circuit riders spread the gospel throughout the American backcountry, planting churches throughout the opening territory.

In the decade before the Revolutionary War, there were less than two dozen Methodist churches in America. By the time of the Civil War, there were a thousand times that many. A hundred years later, in the 1960s, our denomination claimed over 11 million members.

Unfortunately, that rapid growth is no longer the story. Over the last four decades, along with many other denominations, The United Methodist Church has experienced significant decline. Our beloved church now has less than eight million members in the United States. Many younger adults show little interest in the church. In fact, some even express a negative view of Christians.

The first Christians were known for their love. The early North African church father Tertullian is often quoted in this regard from a letter he wrote to the Roman authorities in AD 197, known as *Apologeticus*. In this letter, he sought to defend the church in the face of harsh antagonism and injustice. He described Christian beliefs and practices in great detail, defended the religion's opposition to idolatry, and explained why Christianity was a positive asset for the Empire.

Tertullian's extensive letter is 50 chapters long; the famous quote is found in Chapter 39. Tertullian offered that it was mainly the deeds of love that branded the Christians of his generation. In fact, he insisted they were even willing to die for one another.

The early Christians were not only known for their love of one another. Sociologist of religion and professor Rodney Stark has written about how a disparate, disorganized band of 12 disciples grew into a powerful movement of more than six million believers in less than 200 years.[1]

Stark maintained the early Christians gained a reputation for taking care of neighbors and even loving their enemies. When the plagues struck, many Christians risked their lives to care for the sick. They nursed the ill and elderly, who were sometimes abandoned by their pagan neighbors.

What kind of reputation do Christians have today in America? Are we putting the most effort where Jesus put his efforts? Is our reputation based more on what we are against than who we are for? Are we still known for caring for society's most vulnerable? Are we best known for feeding the hungry and caring for the poor? Certainly, many Christians are still doing these things, but is it where we are creating the most noise or making the greatest impact?

Jesus was clear about what should define us. This lesson takes us back to what Jesus said is most important.

613 Commandments in a Couple of Sentences

Matthew 22:35-36 reports a Pharisee, "a legal expert," set out to test Jesus by asking, "Teacher, what is the greatest commandment in the Law?" His intent was to trick Jesus, much like the Pharisees were trying to do on another occasion when they asked Jesus about paying taxes: "They sent some of the Pharisees and supporters of Herod to trap him in his words. They came to him and said, 'Teacher, we know that you're genuine and you don't worry about what people think. You don't show favoritism but teach God's way as it really is. Does the Law allow people to pay taxes to Caesar or not? Should we pay taxes or not?' " (Mark 12:13-14).

They hoped Jesus would answer in a way that would get him into serious trouble with the Roman authorities. If not, perhaps he would at least give an answer with which his potential followers would be unhappy.

It's not altogether clear just how the lawyer in this account from Matthew's Gospel hoped to trick or "test" Jesus. Not that I have counted, but I'm told there are over 600 commandments in the Old Testament. In fact, Jewish tradition has maintained there are exactly 613 commandments, or *mitzvot*, in the Hebrew Bible. (*Mitzvot* is the plural of *mitzvah*, which is Hebrew for "commandment.")

Jewish tradition insisted that all 613 commandments were equal in importance. Perhaps the lawyer was hoping to get Jesus to suggest one was more significant than another or make some other unpopular statement.

It is interesting Matthew turned Mark's version of this encounter into a story of controversy. In Mark Gospel, which is considered an earlier account by most modern Bible scholars, the lawyer was not trying to trick or test Jesus, but rather seems to have been honestly seeking Jesus' opinion (Mark 12:32-33). And "when Jesus saw that he had answered with wisdom, he said to him, 'You aren't far from God's kingdom' " (Mark 12:23).

If you had to condense your understanding of your Christian faith into one sentence, what would you say? What defines or describes a Christian for you?

The *Shema*

We find this encounter between Jesus and the lawyer in Luke's Gospel, too. According to Luke's account, Jesus didn't actually answer the lawyer's question. Instead, he responded with his own questions: "What is written in the Law? How do you interpret it?" (Luke 10:26). In Luke's account, it is the lawyer who quoted what Christians have come to call the Great Commandments.

However, these now-familiar words did not originate with Jesus nor with the lawyer in Luke's account. Jesus and the lawyer were quoting from Deuteronomy 6:5: "Love the LORD with all your heart, all your being, and all your strength" and Leviticus 19:18, "You must not take revenge nor hold a grudge against any of your people; instead, you must love your neighbor as yourself, I am the LORD."

Deuteronomy 6:4-5 is the first part of what Jews call the *Shema*. Jesus and the lawyer who questioned him, and in fact all of the scribes and Pharisees, would have known these words by heart. Observant Jews traditionally recite the *Shema* each morning and each evening. The first line of the *Shema* (Deuteronomy 6:4) is usually translated in English, "Hear O Israel, the LORD is our God, the LORD is One." The *Shema* is only one of two prayers commanded in the Torah, the other being grace after meals.

The *Shema* invites us to explore ways we can stamp our devotion to God onto every part of our lives.

How do you best express your love for God?

Love Your Neighbor

The second, but necessarily interconnected, greatest commandment is to love our neighbors. Perhaps the best way to express our love for God is to love our neighbor, and Jesus told and showed us how. Jesus affirmed what we find in the Old Testament; and when it comes to loving our neighbors, he broadened its definition. Luke's version of Jesus' conversation with the lawyer helps us at this point by relating one of the most well-known parables in the Bible.

We have already seen the great commandments are found in all three of the Synoptic Gospels: Matthew, Mark, and Luke. The legal expert would have been extremely familiar with Deuteronomy 6 and Leviticus 19. However, something apparently bothered him. Perhaps he had heard Jesus say something that made him wonder if Jesus was giving a new interpretation of Leviticus 19:18. Was Jesus suggesting a new and different understanding of just who our neighbors are?

Luke added to his account of Jesus's conversation with the legal expert: "But the legal expert wanted to prove that he was right so he said to Jesus, 'And who is my neighbor?' " (Luke 10:29). Jesus responded by telling the story of the good Samaritan.

In this legendary story, Jesus talked about a Jewish man who was attacked, robbed, and left for dead on the side of the road. A priest and a Levite happened upon him but passed by on the opposite side of the road, unwilling to help. Finally, a Samaritan, from a people hated by most Jews, came upon the injured man. The Samaritan dressed the injured man's wounds, took him to an inn, cared for him, and left sufficient funds with the innkeeper to continue the care.

By using the example of a hated Samaritan, Jesus did indeed give a whole new interpretation to Leviticus 19:18. The phrase "your people" found in this verse was always understood by the Jews as referring to their fellow Jewish neighbors. Jesus taught we should treat all others as we treat our own family and those in our immediate circle of friends.

Moreover, Jesus actually taught something even more radical. In the Sermon on the Mount, Jesus said, "You have heard that it was said, You must love your neighbor and hate your enemy. But I say to you, love your enemies and pray for those who harass you. . . . If you love only those who love you, what reward do you have? . . . Therefore, just as your heavenly Father is complete in showing love to everyone, so also you must be complete" (Matthew

5:43-48). This is, of course, a lot easier said than done. We need the Spirit of Jesus Christ in order to love like this. Jesus made this clear as recorded in John 15.

Doing nothing is not an option, as other biblical teachings make clear. Fulfilling the greatest commandments calls for us to make every action a testimony to our faith and every activity an opportunity to be mindful of our relationship with God and others.

What changes do you need to make in your attitudes and feelings in order to love your neighbors as Jesus called us to love?

Putting Love Into Practice

What does this look like in real life? Paul tried to explain this in his letter to the Christians in Rome (Romans 13:8-10). The Book of James insists we are commanded by Christ to love everyone, especially the poor, the vulnerable, the marginalized, and the disenfranchised (James 2:1-4, 8).

Recent events in our nation have highlighted deep divisions that have existed for a long time. Well-meaning people of faith on all sides of various issues can sometimes be drawn into using unkind and unloving language and mischaracterizations of those with whom they disagree. Rather than being known only for what we are against, our faith compels us to join with God in life-giving words and actions.

The spiritual practice we are encouraged to engage during the lessons in this unit relates to our testimony in word and deed. Matthew's Gospel concludes with the commissioning of the disciples. We are told after Jesus' resurrection, he instructed his disciples to meet him on a certain mountain in Galilee. There he told them, "I've received all authority in heaven and on earth. Therefore, go and make disciples of all nations, baptizing them in the name of the Father and of the Son and of the Holy Spirit, teaching them to obey everything that I've commanded you. Look, I myself will be with you every day until the end of this present age" (Matthew 28:18-20).

We are included in that commission, and we help fulfill it by what we say and by what we do, by how we love God and love others. Perhaps these familiar words from Edgar Guest's poem "Sermons We See" can challenge us.

"I'd rather see a sermon than hear one any day;
I'd rather one should walk with me than merely tell the way.
The eye's a better pupil and more willing than the ear,
Fine counsel is confusing, but example's always clear;
And the best of all the preachers are the men who live their creeds,
For to see good put in action is what everybody needs."[2]

Dear God, thank you for loving us with an everlasting, unconditional love. Teach us to love others as you have loved us. We are grateful for those who have shared your love with us. Teach us how to effectively share your love in word and deed; in Jesus' name. Amen.

[1]From *The Rise of Christianity: How the Obscure, Marginal, Jesus Movement Became the Dominant Religious Force* (HarperSanFrancisco, 1997).
[2]From "Sermons We See," by Edgar Guest (*goodreads.com/quotes/979349-i-d-rather-see-a-sermon -than-hear-one-any-day*).

The Spiritual Practice of Testimony

The sentiment "Preach the gospel at all times. If necessary, use words" has been historically attributed to St. Francis of Assisi, though there is no definitive evidence that he actually ever said this. As a preacher and a teacher of the Bible, I've always taken to heart another maxim my mother taught me when I was young: "Actions speak louder than words."

A third adage I learned at an early age has also guided my life, particularly my vocation as a pastor: "Practice what you preach." My sermons and Bible lessons will have little impact on others if there is too much dissonance between what I say and what I do. I can't just talk the talk without making a genuine effort to walk the walk.

Of course, there is a sense in which every Christian is, indeed, called to preach the gospel at all times. The church has always understood the Great Commission Jesus gave his disciples as a mission assignment meant for every Christian.

The reality is we shouldn't and we mustn't choose between a testimony of words and a testimony of deeds. At times, it is necessary to use words. No matter how much we love and serve others, it will never bring them into a personal relationship with God through Jesus Christ unless we tell them about Jesus at some point.

Our lessons in this unit encourage us to develop our personal testimonies in word and deed. When we do, we demonstrate our love for God and for others, point to the light and love of God, and obey the Great Commission.

What will you do this week to live your testimony of personal faith in Jesus Christ? What will you say?

Focal Passage: Matthew 5:14-16

Background Text: Matthew 5:1-16

Purpose Statement: To explore how our actions make God's glory and love for the world evident

Matthew 5:14-16

¹⁴You are the light of the world. A city on top of a hill can't be hidden. ¹⁵Neither do people light a lamp and put it under a basket. Instead, they put it on top of a lampstand, and it shines on all who are in the house. ¹⁶In the same way, let your light shine before people, so they can see the good things you do and praise your Father who is in heaven.

Key Verse: "In the same way, let your light shine before people, so they can see the good things you do and praise your Father who is in heaven" (Matthew 5:16).

Ray Pritchard tells a story about a little boy who asked his mother one day in church, "Mom, who are those people in the window?" She responded, "Those are the saints." The boy pondered this deeply for a few moments, then whispered, "Oh, I know who the saints are. They're the ones who let the light in."

There is a sense in which the child in Pritchard's story had it right, but in a way he didn't intend. Saints are indeed those God calls to let the light in. In that understanding, all who have placed their faith in Jesus Christ are the saints.

When many people think of saints, they think about people who are particularly holy or virtuous. Roman Catholics generally understand the word to refer to someone who has died and is in heaven, has met specific criteria, and has been officially recognized and canonized by the church.

In the Bible, the word *saint* refers to someone who is sanctified, set apart, consecrated, declared sacred. This, then, includes all who seek to live in a personal relationship with God through Jesus Christ. For example, Paul began his letter to the church at Rome with this greeting: "To all God's beloved in Rome, who are called to be saints" (Romans 1:7, NRSV).

The word translated "saints" here is the Greek word *hagios*. This word means "holy, sacred, separated from ordinary or common usage, and committed to God." Depending on the context, the word is sometimes also translated "holy."

The CEB renders Romans 1:7, "To those in Rome who are dearly loved by God and called to be *God's people*" (italics added). In other words, according to Paul, all sincere followers of Jesus Christ are considered saints. Because of our relationship with Jesus Christ, we all have the calling and the capacity to "let the light in" for those people and places in darkness.

The author of Luke–Acts also clearly had this understanding. For example, he wrote, "But Ananias answered, 'Lord, I have heard from many about this man, how much evil he has done to your saints in Jerusalem'" (Acts 9:13, NRSV). Referring to all the people in that region, he wrote, "Now as Peter went here and there among all the believers, he came down also to the saints living in Lydda" (Acts 9:32, NRSV).

Jesus said, "You are the light of the world" (Matthew 5:14). The light that emanates from us is the reflected light of Jesus, much in the way the moon reflects the light of the sun.

The author of the Gospel of John began that work with a beautiful introduction: "In the beginning was the Word and the Word was with God and the Word was God. . . . What came into being through the Word was life, and life was the light for all people. The light shines in the darkness, and darkness doesn't extinguish the light" (John 1:1, 3-5). John 8:12 quotes Jesus saying, "I am the light of the world. Whoever follows me won't walk in darkness but will have the light of life."

Jesus' exclamation that we are the light of the world invites us to explore how our actions make God's glory and love for the world evident. While God's glory may be made evident through creation, God's lovingkindness and concern for justice is often most visible when those who profess faith in God make God's love and justice evident.

The Sermon on the Mount

As we noted in an earlier lesson, most modern scholars believe the Book of Mark was the first of the four Gospels written. A few years after it was penned, the author of

Matthew composed his expanded version of the gospel story. He took Mark's account and framed it with a genealogy and birth narrative at the beginning and post-Resurrection appearances at the end. He then added five blocks of teaching material. While the Book of Mark emphasizes what Jesus did, Matthew adds these five major sections that report what Jesus said and taught.

We know the first of these five discourses as the Sermon on the Mount, and the few but powerful verses of our Focal Passage fall within this. While Matthew presents this material (Chapters 5–7) as a "sermon" Jesus gave on a mountaintop, it seems much more likely the material is actually a collection of Jesus' sayings. It is not a random collection, however, but rather a carefully crafted summary of Jesus' overarching message.

The Sermon on the Mount begins with the Beatitudes, which upon first reading seem strange at best, because Jesus identifies blessed or happy people as "those who are regarded as troubled and unfortunate. . . . This alerts us to the topsy-turvy nature of Jesus' teaching. It shows us who experiences well-being and contentment under God's rule rather than according to normal social conventions. In this way, each of these statements declares as happy those people ordinarily regarded as living miserable lives and provides them with an assurance in the form of a promise."[1]

Together, the characteristics Jesus identified in these statements affirm that people who are blessed and happy know God is the source of their help and hope, and they trust God to save and restore them. They believe God can and will restore order and justice and come to their defense.

Beginning with Matthew 5:7, Jesus' emphasis shifts from the needs of God's people to the ways they live their lives in whatever circumstances they find themselves. God's people have received mercy, so they graciously show mercy to others in need. They have "pure hearts" (verse 8) and are honest and sincere instead of deceitful. As children of God, followers of Jesus, they "make peace" (verse 9). Because they are in right relationship with God and with others, they have a sense of complete well-being and work to help achieve peace in the lives of other people and situations characterized by poor relationships and hostility.

People who live in this way live differently in the world. They redefine what it means to thrive and succeed and prosper, and they want others to experience this life, too. We who follow Jesus Christ allow him to transform our emotions, beliefs, and actions. The light of Jesus Christ changes us from deep within, we learn to see things from God's perspective, and we become agents through which God's light can shine.

Matthew made clear by his choice of what he included in this collection of sayings that Jesus was interested in how his followers behaved, not just what they believed. He insisted, "Unless your righteousness is greater than the righteousness of the legal experts and the Pharisees, you will never enter the kingdom of heaven" (verse 20).

How do your thoughts, words, and actions align with the Beatitudes? In what areas do you see the need for additional growth?

Salt, Yeast, Fire, and Light

The late Quaker theologian and author Elton Trueblood (1900-1994) often emphasized the idea "You cannot go to church; you are the church wherever you go." He also pointed out Jesus often used the metaphors of salt, light, yeast, and fire to describe the nature of God's kingdom. All of these images are characterized by their penetrating nature and their ability to transform that which they infuse. The church is called to go into the world and be a transforming agent.

One of my earliest recollections is my family's salt box. Electricity had come to our "neck of the woods" just a few months before I was born. My parents had purchased one of those newfangled electric iceboxes, but much of the pork we butchered on our farm was still preserved in the smokehouse and the salt box.

In the verse that precedes our Focal Passage, Jesus declared, "You are the salt of the earth. But if salt loses its saltiness, how will it become salty again? It's good for nothing except to be thrown away and trampled under people's feet" (Matthew 5:13). Salt not only improves the taste of our food, it also serves as a preservative.

Matthew 13 records a series of short parables Jesus told. One of these is found in Matthew 13:33: "He told them another parable: 'The kingdom of heaven is like yeast, which a woman took and hid in a bushel of wheat flour until the yeast had worked its way through all the dough.'"

This parable is also found in Luke 13:20-21, and in both Gospels it follows the parable of the mustard seed. "[Jesus] told another parable to them: 'The kingdom of heaven is like a mustard seed that someone took and planted in his field. It's the smallest of all seeds. But when it's grown, it's the largest of all vegetable plants. It becomes a tree so that the birds in the sky come and nest in its branches'" (Matthew 13:31-32).

Much like salt, it only takes a small amount of yeast to make the bread rise. Paul declared, "Don't you know that a tiny grain of yeast makes a whole batch of dough rise?" (1 Corinthians 5:6). God's work through Jesus Christ did indeed begin with a small band of ragtag followers of dubious abilities and accomplishments who grew into the most powerful force the world has ever known. One person and God can make a difference. A small group of committed followers of Christ can change the world.

Fire is another powerful metaphor, and we find it used numerous times throughout Scripture. John the Baptist proclaimed, "I baptize with water those of you who have changed your hearts and lives. The one who is coming after me is stronger than I am. I'm not worthy to carry his sandals. He will baptize you with the Holy Spirit and with fire" (Matthew 3:11). Of course, when we think of fire, we often think of destruction. A single spark can spread and cause immense destruction. But fire is also used to refine and purify.

Our Focal Passage for this lesson focuses on the metaphor of light. Again, like salt, yeast, and fire, even a small amount goes a long way. For several years now, I have placed this at the end of all emails I send: "One small candle can dispel the darkness." The darker it is, the less light it takes to make a difference. Moreover, as John's Gospel reminds us, "The light shines in the darkness, and the darkness doesn't extinguish the light" (John 1:5).

Of the images of salt, yeast, fire, and light, which best communicates to you your role as Jesus' follower? Which challenges you the most?

The Light of the World

The idea that God's people are to be the light of the world begins early in our history. Genesis 12 relates the story of Abram's divine calling. There we read, "I will bless those who bless you, those who curse you I will curse; all the families of the earth will be blessed because of you" (Genesis 12:3).

Second Samuel 21:17 refers to David as "Israel's lamp." The prophet Isaiah called God's people to remember their role in God's work in the world: "He said: It is not enough, since you are my servant, to raise up the tribes of Jacob and to bring back the survivors of Israel. Hence, I will also appoint you as light to the nations so that my salvation may reach to the end of the earth" (Isaiah 49:6).

Luke 2 records when Joseph and Mary took the young Jesus to the Temple to be consecrated, they met Simeon. Simeon had been waiting for years to see the Messiah. He took Jesus in his arms and recalled a passage from Isaiah.

Speaking of Israel, the prophet wrote, "I, the LORD, have called you in righteousness; I will take hold of your hand. I will keep you and will make you to be a covenant for the people and a light for the Gentiles, to open eyes that are blind, to free captives from prison and to release from the dungeon those who sit in darkness" (Isaiah 42:6-7, NIV).

This is our calling as Christians. Our mission is to shine God's light in the darkness, to share divine love, and to serve others in Jesus' name. The Jesus who said, "While I am in the world, I am the light of the world" (John 9:5), also declared, "You are the light of the world. A city on top of a hill can't be hidden. Neither do people light a lamp and put it under a basket. Instead, they put it on top of a lampstand, and it shines on all who are in the house. In the same way, let your light shine before people, so they can see the good things you do and praise your Father who is in heaven" (Matthew 5:14-16).

How can we do this? How can we be the ones who "let the light in"? Jesus said, " 'Whoever wants to be first must be least of all and the servant of all' " (Mark 9:35). The apostle Paul encouraged the Christians in Galatia writing, "You were called to freedom, brothers and sisters; only don't let this freedom be an opportunity to indulge your selfish impulses, but serve each other through love" (Galatians 5:13).

Remember the spiritual practice we are encouraged to engage during this unit of lessons involves our testimony in word and deed. In 1 Peter 2:9, we read, "But you are a chosen race, a royal priesthood, a holy nation, a people who are God's own possession. You have become this people so that you may speak of the wonderful acts of the one who called you out of darkness into his amazing light."

We are called to shed God's light back into the darkness from whence we have come.

How can you reflect the light of Jesus Christ into the dark spaces you encounter this week? Is there some issue about which you need to speak out? Do you know someone who needs to know more about how God can bring them healing and wholeness?

Dear God, we pray today for the gifts of wisdom and vision to discern your will and hear your call; for the gift of faith to overcome our doubts; and for the gift of courage to keep us single-minded in our commitment to your cause so that we will faithfully carry out whatever mission you give us. Fill our hearts with the love and compassion that will motivate us to shed your light; in Jesus' name we pray. Amen.

[1]From *The CEB Study Bible*, New Testament; page 12.

Informing, Transforming Faith

Focal Passage: James 1:19-27
Background Text: Same
Purpose Statement: To better understand the relationship between belief and practice

James 1:19-27

¹⁹Know this, my dear brothers and sisters: everyone should be quick to listen, slow to speak, and slow to grow angry. ²⁰This is because an angry person doesn't produce God's righteousness. ²¹Therefore, with humility, set aside all moral filth and the growth of wickedness, and welcome the word planted deep inside you—the very word that is able to save you.

²²You must be doers of the word and not only hearers who mislead themselves. ²³Those who hear but don't do the word are like those who look at their faces in a mirror. ²⁴They look at themselves, walk away, and immediately forget what they were like. ²⁵But there are those who study the perfect law, the law of freedom, and continue to do it. They don't listen and then forget, but they put it into practice in their lives. They will be blessed in whatever they do.

²⁶If those who claim devotion to God don't control what they say, they mislead themselves. Their devotion is worthless. ²⁷True devotion, the kind that is pure and faultless before God the Father, is this: to care for

orphans and widows in their difficulties and to keep the world from contaminating us.

Key Verse: "You must be doers of the word and not only hearers who mislead themselves" (James 1:22).

I confess at one time I was pretty bad about ignoring the instructions that come with items that must be assembled. But several years ago, I purchased something that permanently changed my approach. Its assembly seemed quite straightforward, so I quickly tossed aside the instructions and went to work. It took quite a while, but I made steady progress. I thought I was practically finished when I hit a snag.

Because I had not put the parts together in the proper order, it was impossible to proceed without disassembling most of them. To make matters worse, some of the parts had been designed to snap together, and I could not disconnect them without breaking them! It took me much longer to complete the assembly than it should have. Moreover, the final product was far less satisfactory than it would have been had I first assembled it according to its instructions.

Instructions have no value to us unless we follow them. God has provided in the Bible a fantastic instruction book. It gives us great guidelines and provides specific directions that tell us how to live in right relationship with God and with one another while we find joy, meaning, and purpose in life. It only makes sense, then, if we expend great effort reading, studying, and even memorizing this book, we will also follow its instructions.

Pastor and author Stuart Briscoe recalled a time when he was teaching a group of Christians the principles he recommends for Bible study. He demonstrated how he identifies the promises and the commands in Scripture and what to do with them. After explaining everything, he asked as a way of review and to assess their comprehension, "Now, what do you do with the commands?" One woman raised her hand and said, "I underline them in blue."

Of course, that wasn't the answer Pastor Briscoe had in mind. Once we identify God's commands, we should seek to obey them. It's not enough to read and study the Bible and learn a great deal about what it says. If we fail to apply the Bible's teachings to our lives, we miss the point.

The author of the little book of James insists, "You must be doers of the word and not only hearers who mislead themselves. Those who hear but don't do the word are like those who look at their faces in a mirror. They look at themselves, walk away, and immediately forget what they were like" (James 1:22-24). Those who put into practice Scripture's teachings, he said, "will be blessed in whatever they do" (verse 25).

James and the General Epistles

When we study a particular passage of Scripture, it's always important to understand its context and how it fits in with the rest of the biblical narrative. As we move from this lesson into the letter from James, we find it toward the end of the New Testament among what are known as the General Epistles. You recall, of course, the first section of the New Testament includes the four Gospels, which deal with Jesus' life and teachings.

The second section of the New Testament includes the Book of Acts and the Pauline Letters. The Book of Acts, written by the same author as was the Book of Luke, focuses on Peter and Paul and describes the expansion of the early church. It particularly seeks to explain how Christianity transitioned from a Jewish base to include Gentiles.

Most biblical scholars consider the books of Romans, 1 and 2 Corinthians, Galatians, Philippians, Philemon, and 1 Thessalonians to have been written by the apostle Paul. Some question whether he actually penned the books of Ephesians and Colossians as well as the pastoral letters of 1 and 2 Timothy and Titus, although the opening verse in each of those books identifies the writer as Paul.

The third section of the New Testament includes books often referred to as the General Epistles. These letters were originally addressed to the church at-large rather than to specific congregations and include James; 1 and 2 Peter; 1, 2, and 3 John; and Jude.

The General Epistles tend to deal with the practical matters of living as Christians in the hostile environment in which Jesus' early followers found themselves. Two important themes run through these books. First, we can trust God to take care of the faithful. Second, Christians must be faithful and obedient to God's laws and commands.

Of course, the most important of these commandments involve loving God with all our heart, soul, mind, and strength and loving our neighbors as ourselves. One way God takes care of us is rooted in this commandment to care for one another.

Even though these books are commonly referred to as epistles, this term does not fully describe the various literary forms comprised by these texts. The Book of James is of particular interest in this regard. The book certainly begins like a letter: "From James, a slave of God and of the Lord Jesus Christ. To the twelve tribes who are scattered outside the land of Israel" (James 1:1). The problem is no one knows exactly to whom this refers. Moreover, there is much in the rest of the book that does not actually read like a letter.

One tradition has held that the book was written by James the brother of Jesus. However, given the wide-ranging content, vocabulary, and writing style, this seems quite unlikely, though it may indeed have some kind of historical connection with him. James includes moral instruction that sometimes parallels the moral philosophy of the Greco-Roman culture, but it also seems to have an even greater Jewish flavor.

Some have insisted the Book of James has no general theme but is simply a collection of brief moral dictums often connected by some insignificant relationship. However, there is one overarching motif that runs throughout the book. That motif is perhaps best summarized by our Key Verse, "You must be doers of the word and not only hearers who mislead themselves" (James 1:22). When we hear and do God's word, we join in God's work in the world. When we do not, we cannot be a part of that work.

In what ways do we deceive ourselves when we hear God's Word but fail to obey or apply it?

Listening and Speaking, Hearing and Doing

Our focal passage, James 1:19-27, clearly emphasizes three important things: listening carefully and speaking thoughtfully (James 1:19-21); hearing and doing God's Word (verses 22-25); and what true devotion involves (26-27).

Mark Twain famously said, "It ain't those parts of the Bible that I can't understand that bother me, it is the parts that I do understand." Our text this week is one those passages for me. It's not hard to understand what James is telling us. It is hard to do it. However, if we complained to James about this, what do you think he would say?

As we noted above, James tended to jump from one subject to another with tenuous connections. Sometimes it was simply a play on words. In verse 19, he says we "should be quick to listen, slow to speak, and slow to grow angry." He explained that anger doesn't lead to righteousness. With two words (in the English), he recommended humility; then in one phrase, he warned against our innate wickedness. He finished the sentence encouraging everyone to "welcome the word planted deep inside you—the very word that is able to save you" (verse 21).

In the next sentence, James picks up the term "word" and proclaimed, "You must be doers of the word and not hearers who mislead themselves." Reading these four verses might remind us of a couple of maxims. The first is, "God gave us two ears and one mouth. We should listen twice as much as we talk." The second is Benjamin Franklin's famous quote, "Well done is better than well said."

James said people who look at God's Word but immediately forget (ignore) what they have read are like those who look at themselves in the mirror but "immediately forget what they look like" (verse 23). He might have said, "They let it go in one ear and out the other."

James returned to this emphasis on behavior in the second chapter where he drilled down on concern. There he asked, "My brothers and sisters, what good is it if people say they have faith but do nothing to show it? Claiming to have faith can't save anyone, can it?" (2:14). A few verses later, he reiterated, "So you see that a person is shown to be righteous through faithful actions and not through faith alone" (2:24).

Bible students sometimes point out that Paul and James seem to have been at odds in their teaching. Faith alone, not works, was Paul's theme. Faith without works, James said, is useless. Who was right? *The CEB Study Bible* offers this helpful distinction and assures us we don't have to choose sides:

"Some have argued James' teaching contradicts Paul's teaching. However, Paul and James have different concerns. For Paul, works of the Jewish Law do not lead to faith and justification. Such a view would deny the importance of Jesus Christ, who alone attained our salvation (Gal 2:15-16). Paul does not deny the need for believers, once they have the gift of faith, to express their faith by doing good deeds (e.g. Rom 2:6; Phil 1:21-22; Eph 4:12). James is concerned that faith be alive by responding with good deeds (Jas 2:14-26). In fact, he expresses what Jesus says in the Sermon on the Mount, 'Not everybody who says to me, "Lord, Lord," will get into the kingdom of heaven. Only those who do the will of my Father who is in heaven will enter' (Matt 7:21)."[1]

How does your faith inform the way you listen? the way you speak? What is the difference between the faith that doesn't result in changed behavior and faith that results in a transformed life?

True Devotion

In James 1:26, James returned to the matter of speech: "If those who claim devotion to God don't control what they say, they mislead themselves. Their devotion is worthless." We demonstrate our commitment and devotion to God by our actions. And if we can't control the words that come out of our mouths, our claims to devotion don't mean anything.

Beyond what we say and how we say it, James said that we show our devotion to God in two other ways: by caring "for orphans and widows in their difficulties," and by keeping "the world from contaminating us" (James 1:27). Anything that opposes God has no place in the life of a Christian.

Similar to his reference to looking into a mirror in verse 23, James again forces us to turn the spotlight into the interior of our hearts and lives. To what degree do we control our speech? How do we help those who are most vulnerable and in need? James is clear. He doesn't suggest that a compromise is possible. He challenges us to look inward, honestly, and then make a choice. Our choices reveal where our devotion lies.

In an earlier lesson, we considered part of the Sermon on the Mount as recorded in Matthew and what Jesus tells us about how we are to live. I love the way Eugene Peterson paraphrases Matthew 5:48 in *The Message*. "In a word, what I'm saying is, Grow up. You're kingdom subjects. Now live like it. Live out your God-created identity. Live generously and graciously toward others, the way God lives toward you."

Jesus was talking about spiritual maturity. A disciple strives to continually grow in Christ, seeking to become more like Jesus every day. This growth is not an option for the Christian. To fail to grow is to die.

The spiritual practice we are encouraged to engage as we study the lessons in this unit concerns our testimony, what we say and what we do. To guide your practice this week, ask yourself this question at the end of each day: "What did I do or not do today that proclaimed Jesus' message of love, forgiveness, and service to others?"

How do you determine the degree of your faith commitment? What do you do to make it deeper and stronger?

Which is more difficult for you—controlling your speech or transforming your actions in ways that serve God and others?

Dear God, we know that your love never fails, your blessings never cease, and your grace is always sufficient. Help us to recognize that knowing your word is useless unless we put it into practice; in Jesus' name we pray. Amen.

[1]From *The CEB Study Bible*, New Testament; page 457.

Focal Passage: Matthew 28:16-20
Background Text: Same
Purpose Statement: To explore what it means to make disciples

Matthew 28:16-20

[16]Now the eleven disciples went to Galilee, to the mountain where Jesus told them to go. [17]When they saw him, they worshipped him, but some doubted. [18]Jesus came near and spoke to them, "I've received all authority in heaven and on earth. [19]Therefore, go and make disciples of all nations, baptizing them in the name of the Father and of the Son and of the Holy Spirit, [20]teaching them to obey everything that I've commanded you. Look, I myself will be with you every day until the end of this present age."

Key Verse: "Therefore, go and make disciples of all nations, baptizing them in the name of the Father and of the Son and of the Holy Spirit" (Matthew 28:19).

On my personal website (*thetransformativechurch. org*), I offer a contemporary parable about a man who developed a formula for a superior machine oil. He was able to convince a group of investors to back his new company. When the factory was completed, the man invited his investors for a tour of the new facility. They were fascinated with the whole operation. Finally, someone asked about the shipping department. "Oh," the man explained, "we don't have a shipping department. We use all the oil we manufacture right here on the site to keep all of our machines running at top efficiency."

I wonder how many churches have something in common with this man's oil factory. If we looked at our church budgets, how much of our resources (money, time, and people) would we discover are spent on institutional maintenance rather than on the mission and ministry to which we are called by Jesus Christ?

Our lessons this quarter have reminded us that the greatest commandments are to love God and love our neighbors. This love is not about having a nice warm feeling about those who live next door; it is about how we treat others, even our enemies.

First John 3:18 says, "Little children, let's not love with words or speech but with action and truth." John 15:1-2 reads, "I am the true vine and my Father is the vineyard keeper. He removes any of my branches that don't produce fruit, and he trims any branch that produces fruit so that it will produce even more fruit."

In Matthew 25, Jesus says in the end, we will be judged by how we have treated others, not what we have claimed to believe. He instructed us to take up our cross and follow him, which certainly involves helping the poor and oppressed. Jesus announced at the outset of his ministry,

"The Spirit of the Lord is on me, because he has anointed me to proclaim good news to the poor. He has sent me to proclaim freedom for the prisoners and recovery of sight for the blind, to set the oppressed free, to proclaim the year of the Lord's favor" (Luke 4:18-19).

Our Focal Passage marks the first time Jesus' disciples have appeared on the scene in Matthew's Gospel since they ran away during his arrest. Matthew assumed they had come to faith in the resurrected Jesus not because they had seen him, but because of the testimony of the women who had seen Him. In this brief encounter, Jesus charged his disciples with what would be their lifelong task.

Jesus called them to "make disciples of all nations." That is Jesus' call to us, too. If we take Jesus' call seriously, we must ask ourselves and our churches: Are we sincere disciples who are intentionally making more disciples of Jesus Christ? How does the way our church invests resources reflect our commitment to discipleship?

Are we investing in mission and ministry, or are we, like the machine oil company described above, keeping our resources to ourselves? Do we measure the church's success by the size of our budgets or the number who attend on Sunday, or by our faithfulness to the mission God has given us?

Who Is a Disciple?

Before Jesus told the disciples what they should do, he established the basis for his instructions: "I've received all authority in heaven and on earth" (Matthew 28:18).

The now-resurrected Jesus rules heaven and earth. And with that authority, Jesus gave his instructions to "make disciples of all nations, baptizing them in the name of the Father and of the Son and of the Holy Spirit, teaching them to obey everything that I've commanded you" (verses 19-20).

The opportunity to follow Jesus, to be his disciple, is open to everyone, people in "all nations." The call that was once extended to individual fishermen, a tax collector, and others who formed the original Twelve was now extended to all people everywhere. And baptism was the identifying mark.

Based on his authority, Jesus extended authority to the disciples not only to baptize but to teach. The result? Those who become dedicated followers of Jesus Christ seek to discover God's purpose for their lives, and work to fulfill that purpose.[1]

Of course, a disciple is a believer. However, a disciple is not someone who simply believes certain facts about Jesus or believes in certain religious doctrines. A disciple is one who understands that trusting in Jesus leads to changed behavior. A disciple is willing to sacrifice for the sake of serving. Matthew 16:24 reports, "Jesus said to his disciples, 'All who want to come after me must say no to themselves, take up their cross, and follow me.' "

Christian disciples seek to live by the principles and ethical precepts taught in the Bible. According to the

Gospel of John, Jesus said, "If you love me, you will keep my commandments" (John 14:15).

Perhaps the best and briefest way to explain what it means to be a disciple is to say that a disciple is a person who is committed to keeping the Great Commandments: "*You must love the Lord your God with all your heart, with all your being*, and with all your mind. . . . *You must love your neighbor as you love yourself*"—and helping to fulfill the Great Commission—"to go and make disciples of all nations, baptizing them in the name of the Father and of the Son and of the Holy Spirit" (Matthew 22:37, 39; 28:19).

As a disciple of Jesus, what beliefs and behaviors are most important to you? What most characterizes your life as a Christian disciple?

Why Be a Disciple?

Jesus never withheld his expectations when calling followers. He made it clear discipleship comes with a cost. "Whoever doesn't carry their own cross and follow me cannot be my disciple. If one of you wanted to build a tower, wouldn't you first sit down and calculate the cost, to determine whether you have enough money to complete it? . . . In the same way, none of you who are unwilling to give up all of your possessions can be my disciple" (Luke 14:27-28, 33).

Jesus didn't simply ask others to believe in him. He invited them to "take up their cross" and follow him. His was a call to radical discipleship. He was straightforward about the cost but insisted the rewards are worth the investment. These rewards are heavenly and earthly.

In Matthew 25, Jesus warned, "I was hungry and you didn't give me food to eat. I was thirsty and you didn't give me anything to drink. I was a stranger and you didn't welcome me. I was naked and you didn't give me clothes to wear. I was sick and in prison, and you didn't visit me. . . . I assure you that when you haven't done it for one of the least of these, you haven't done it for me" (Matthew 25:42-43, 45).

While most Bible scholars don't think Jesus meant this to say that deeds of love and mercy are the only criteria for judgment, it does suggest that belief of certain theological doctrines without change in behavior is inadequate. Discipleship offers:

- meaning and purpose in life that sustain us regardless of the circumstances (Ephesians 2:10)
- spiritual strength to overcome destructive sin and develop much greater stability (Ephesians 4:11-16)
- opportunities to make a positive impact on the world (Matthew 5:13-16)
- more mature, satisfying relationships
- joy, peace, and contentment
- a much better understanding of success and a greater degree of happiness

What has your decision to follow Jesus as a disciple cost you? What have you gained as a result of this decision?

Why Make Disciples?

Even if we understand there are many benefits of being a follower of Jesus Christ, we might still ask why someone would want to make disciples. Some people insist that religion is a private matter. We may have been told there are three things we shouldn't talk about in "polite company": money, politics, and religion.

But if we believe that being a disciple of Jesus can make an enormous difference in a person's life and even change the world, shouldn't we tell others we care about?

We work to make disciples because we want everyone to find the eternal peace, purpose, joy, and success in life we have found in our relationship with God through Jesus Christ. We also believe the more people who are transformed by their relationship with Jesus, the better our world will be for everyone.

Christians invite others to follow Jesus because Jesus commanded us to do so. We are not obedient disciples of Jesus if we aren't encouraging others to be obedient disciples of Jesus.

If someone asked you why you choose to follow Jesus, how would you respond?

How Are Disciples Made?

How does a person actually become a genuine disciple of Jesus Christ? How do we learn anything? to walk? to tie our shoes? to add and subtract?

We can learn from classroom-style teaching (lectures and sermons), apprenticeship (coaching, mentoring), and imitation (like children learn to speak and internalize customs and conventions of a particular culture). Though the church has primarily used classroom-style teaching in our attempt to develop disciples, is this the most effective method?

Jesus taught and preached to large groups of people at times, but he used other methods as well. He realized many in the crowds abandoned him as soon as they understood he was calling them to make radical changes in their lives. So Jesus spent most of his time mentoring and coaching a specific small group. Jesus knew making a disciple, transforming a life, takes time and commitment. Mature followers of Jesus aren't created overnight. Jesus spent three years mentoring the Twelve.

Apprenticeship is a great way to make disciples, but Jesus actually went beyond that with the Twelve. The most powerful method to transform a life is imitation, and Jesus clearly used this method with them.

A child learns to walk, talk, and conform to certain cultural conventions by imitating those around him. This is, of course, the slowest method of all but the one that transforms. This is why most new members on church rolls come from the children of church members, and this is why we see fewer adult converts. Most adult converts are brought to the church by someone else who has invested a great deal of time and effort in their lives. How many of us are willing to make this kind of investment in others?

The lessons in this unit have encouraged us to pursue the spiritual practice related to our testimony, what we say and what we do. I have found the following steps helpful in my efforts to carry out the Great Commission in word and deed:

- Make a list of your friends, relatives, associates, and neighbors who might benefit from a closer walk with God.
- Develop a profile of each individual, recording what you know about each one.
- Pray regularly for each person on your list.
- Choose three or four on whom you will focus, preferably those who are mostly likely to be receptive and with whom you best relate.
- Be intentional about developing a deeper relationship with each of these. Invite them into your life, and spend more time listening to them than talking.
- Introduce them to other mature Christians who might share common interests.
- Slowly, as appropriate opportunities arise, share your story and how God has made a difference in your life.
- Mentor/coach them. Even if they become professing Christians, stay in relationship with them. Encourage them to develop a relationship with an accountability partner, you or someone else. Check in with them regularly to see how they are doing.

What steps will you take in the coming week that can help someone else become a disciple of Jesus Christ?

Dear God, give us your gift of wisdom to help us overcome our lack of understanding. Give us your gift of peace to help us overcome our chaotic lives. Give us your gift of faith to help us overcome our doubts. Give us your gift of courage to help us overcome the fear that hinders us from loving others and sharing your love that can transform lives and change the world; in Jesus' name we pray. Amen.

[1]From *thetransformativechurch.org*.

Coming Next Quarter

Follow

This spring, our lessons center around the theme "Follow." The writer of the student book lessons is Rita Hays; the teacher book writer is David Mosser. Our lessons fall within two units this quarter instead of three so that we can mark the six weeks of Lent leading up to Easter..

The Mark You Make

Discipleship in Mark's Gospel is often described as the way of the cross because of the repeated emphasis upon following Jesus on the way to Jerusalem and the command to take up one's cross and follow Jesus (Mark 8:34). In these weeks in which we commemorate Jesus' journey to Jerusalem, we give our attention to various aspects of discipleship highlighted in Mark's Gospel. We begin with a lesson that helps us better understand Jesus' identity and follow that with lessons on recognizing fellow disciples along the way, understanding Jesus' upside-down kingdom, deepening our understanding of the relationship between faith and prayer, watching for signs of new creation breaking through, and accepting Jesus' forgiveness when we as his disciples miss the mark. We conclude this unit with a celebration of Jesus' resurrection based on Mark's account of the empty tomb.

The Steps You Take

Creation care has become a prominent topic of discussion in Christian congregations and seminaries during the last couple of decades. While there is disagreement about human responsibility for climate change and to what extent we should limit human activity for the purpose of preservation of endangered species and habitats, Scripture makes clear that God takes pleasure in creation and that our role as stewards requires that we appreciate creation and take our responsibility as stewards seriously. The lessons in this unit lead us to better observe God's beautiful creation, understand why all of God's creation needs sabbath, grow in our understanding of tithing as stewardship of God's resources, acknowledge the limits of our understanding when confronted with the complexities of creation, anticipate God's restoration of creation, and model God's generosity by paying it forward..

CPSIA information can be obtained
at www.ICGtesting.com
Printed in the USA
LVHW040927121121
702955LV00006B/210